A Greek Prose Reading  for Post-Beginners

Unit 2. Philosophy
Plato: *Crito*

With Commentary and
Vocabulary by
MALCOLM CAMPBELL

Bristol Classical Press

First published in 1997 by
Bristol Classical Press
an imprint of
Gerald Duckworth & Co. Ltd
61 Frith Street
London W1V 5TA

Reprinted 1999

A catalogue record for this book is available
from the British Library

ISBN 1-85399-538-X

Typeset by Malcolm Campbell

Printed and bound by Antony Rowe Ltd, Eastbourne

UNIT 2. PHILOSOPHY

CONTENTS

PREFACE

My thanks to John Betts for giving this project a warm reception and for very helpful advice, and to his team at Bristol Classical Press, Jean Scott, Editor, and Graham Douglas in Production, for welcome assistance with typesetting; to my colleagues Professor Stephen Halliwell and Dr Niall Livingstone for taking the time to read the typescripts and for suggesting a number of improvements; to my wife Dorothy for her encouragement, patience and technical help; to my younger son Richard for devoting more than one long evening to explaining to me what I was unable to work out for myself through reading *Macs for Dummies.*

No two teachers of Greek are likely to agree for long on how textbooks of this nature should be formatted, let alone what sort of information, and how much information, they should contain. I have been guided here first and foremost by our own students at St Andrews: I am grateful to them for discussing their difficulties and needs with me, for filling in questionnaires, and for producing some useful feedback on the form and content of earlier drafts of the Lysias and Plato texts. I must thank too a class of Bristol undergraduates whom I have never met, for offering general comment on the Lysias notes circulated to them in 1996 through the kind offices of John Betts and Onno van Nijf.

St Andrews, February 1997   M.C.

GENERAL INTRODUCTION TO THE COURSE

Represented in this course are three of the giants among prose writers of the Classical period, the historian Thucydides, the philosopher Plato, the orator Demosthenes. The same ancient literary critic (Dionysius of Halicarnassus) who called Demosthenes' *Philippic* iii "the greatest of the public orations directed against Philip" also found much to admire in the speeches of Lysias (see M. Edwards and S. Usher, *Greek Orators* I [Warminster, 1985], 128-9). There is certainly much to interest the modern reader in *On the Murder of Eratosthenes*.

In annotating these texts I have tried to keep the needs of three classes of reader constantly in mind:
Students fresh from Beginners courses (whether at University or elsewhere) reading an extended (and undoctored) Greek text for the first time.
Post-A-level (or equivalent) students who wish to consolidate their reading skills.
Postgraduate students who have some Greek but require guidance in reading an historical, oratorical or philosophical text in the original.

Since each unit is self-contained, those with an interest in Socrates, for example, can take on *Crito* right away. But post-Beginners are advised to read the Lysias speech before anything else: it is an excellent starter-text, and for that reason extra help has been given with the verbal systems. For the benefit of those who do choose to take on the course in its entirety the other three components have been given different emphases: in the Plato special attention is paid to the use of particles and particle-combinations, in the Demosthenes (a prime model for the few who still do Greek prose composition) to a number of key differences between Greek and English idiom; the Thucydides approximates more closely to the kind of commentary students will encounter if they carry their Greek studies further, with more extensive coverage of the subject-matter and explicit references to secondary literature. One possible programme, extending over two or three semesters: Lysias, Plato, Demosthenes and/ or Thucydides interspersed with a play of Euripides or Sophocles and a book or two of Homer.

For all four units the layout is essentially the same, and recommendations on study-methods are given in the respective prefaces:
1 Greek text. Observations are made from time to time in the Notes on the constitution of the text, and those who wish to pursue these matters further may consult the following editions, in which a critical apparatus (*apparatus criticus*) is

printed at the bottom of the page, where the editor, communicating in Latin, records variant readings in ancient and mediaeval copies (identified in the "Sigla" prefacing the text itself) and points to places where modern scholars have felt dissatisfied with the transmitted text and considered it necessary to emend:

Lysias, Oxford text by K. Hude (1912), see also the edition by C. Carey (1989), pp.12-13

Plato, Oxford text by E.A. Duke and others (1995)

Demosthenes, Oxford text by S.H. Butcher (1903), Budé text by M. Croiset (1955)

Thucydides, Budé text by J. de Romilly (1967), Oxford text by H.S. Jones and J.E. Powell (2nd edn, 1942).

2 Preliminary remarks on word formation and syntax geared to the text in question. Common to all: a systematic analysis of Perfects/ Pluperfects (usually viewed with dread by post-Beginners, in my experience), and a review of the uses of Subjunctive and Optative.

3 A brief outline of the entire work/ extract.

4 A summary of the content of each block of text.

5 Dedicated vocabularies, broken down into the various parts of speech. The words within each category are arranged alphabetically according to type: in the case of verbs, for example, infinitives in -ειν -εσθαι, then contracted forms -ᾶν -ᾶσθαι/ -εῖν -εῖσθαι/ -οῦν -οῦσθαι, and finally -ναι -σθαι.

6 Notes dealing with language, style and subject-matter.

7 It is envisaged that the material on each of the texts provided here will be topped up by tutors with a course of lectures dealing with author, genre, general background, broad issues and particular problems of interpretation. Those going it alone will find something to suit most tastes in the secondary literature specified in the suggestions for further reading.

ΠΛΑΤΩΝΟΣ
ΚΡΙΤΩΝ

ΣΩΚΡΑΤΗΣ   ΚΡΙΤΩΝ

43a ΣΩ. τί τηνικάδε ἀφῖξαι, ὦ Κρίτων; ἢ οὐ πρῲ ἔτι ἐστίν;
ΚΡ. πάνυ μὲν οὖν.
ΣΩ. πηνίκα μάλιστα;
ΚΡ. ὄρθρος βαθύς.
a5 ΣΩ. θαυμάζω ὅπως ἠθέλησέ σοι ὁ τοῦ δεσμωτηρίου
φύλαξ ὑπακοῦσαι.
ΚΡ. συνήθης ἤδη μοί ἐστιν, ὦ Σώκρατες, διὰ τὸ πολλάκις δεῦρο φοιτᾶν, καί τι καὶ εὐεργέτηται ὑπ᾽ ἐμοῦ.
ΣΩ. ἄρτι δὲ ἥκεις ἢ πάλαι;
a10 ΚΡ. ἐπιεικῶς πάλαι.
43b ΣΩ. εἶτα πῶς οὐκ εὐθὺς ἐπήγειράς με, ἀλλὰ σιγῇ
παρακάθησαι;
ΚΡ. οὐ μὰ τὸν Δία, ὦ Σώκρατες, οὐδ᾽ ἂν αὐτὸς ἤθελον
ἐν τοσαύτῃ τε ἀγρυπνίᾳ καὶ λύπῃ εἶναι, ἀλλὰ καὶ σοῦ
b5 πάλαι θαυμάζω αἰσθανόμενος ὡς ἡδέως καθεύδεις· καὶ
ἐπίτηδές σε οὐκ ἤγειρον ἵνα ὡς ἥδιστα διάγῃς. καὶ πολλάκις μὲν δή σε καὶ πρότερον ἐν παντὶ τῷ βίῳ ηὐδαιμόνισα
τοῦ τρόπου, πολὺ δὲ μάλιστα ἐν τῇ νῦν παρεστώσῃ συμ-
φορᾷ, ὡς ῥᾳδίως αὐτὴν καὶ πρᾴως φέρεις.
b10 ΣΩ. καὶ γὰρ ἄν, ὦ Κρίτων, πλημμελὲς εἴη ἀγανακτεῖν
τηλικοῦτον ὄντα εἰ δεῖ ἤδη τελευτᾶν.
43c ΚΡ. καὶ ἄλλοι, ὦ Σώκρατες, τηλικοῦτοι ἐν τοιαύταις
συμφοραῖς ἁλίσκονται, ἀλλ᾽ οὐδὲν αὐτοὺς ἐπιλύεται ἡ ἡλι-
κία τὸ μὴ οὐχὶ ἀγανακτεῖν τῇ παρούσῃ τύχῃ.
ΣΩ. ἔστι ταῦτα. ἀλλὰ τί δὴ οὕτω πρῲ ἀφῖξαι;
c5 ΚΡ. ἀγγελίαν, ὦ Σώκρατες, φέρων χαλεπήν, οὐ σοί,
ὡς ἐμοὶ φαίνεται, ἀλλ᾽ ἐμοὶ καὶ τοῖς σοῖς ἐπιτηδείοις πᾶσιν
καὶ χαλεπὴν καὶ βαρεῖαν, ἣν ἐγώ, ὡς ἐμοὶ δοκῶ, ἐν τοῖς
βαρύτατ᾽ ἂν ἐνέγκαιμι.
ΣΩ. τίνα ταύτην; ἢ τὸ πλοῖον ἀφῖκται ἐκ Δήλου, οὗ δεῖ
43d ἀφικομένου τεθνάναι με;
ΚΡ. οὔτοι δὴ ἀφῖκται, ἀλλὰ δοκεῖν μέν μοι ἥξει
τήμερον ἐξ ὧν ἀπαγγέλλουσιν ἥκοντές τινες ἀπὸ Σουνίου

κἀι καταλιπόντες ἐκεῖ αὐτό. δῆλον οὖν ἐκ τούτων τῶν
d5 ἀγγέλων ὅτι ἥξει τήμερον, καὶ ἀνάγκη δὴ εἰς αὔριον ἔσται,
ὦ Σώκρατες, τὸν βίον σε τελευτᾶν.
ΣΩ. ἀλλ᾽, ὦ Κρίτων, τύχῃ ἀγαθῇ, εἰ ταύτῃ τοῖς θεοῖς
φίλον, ταύτῃ ἔστω· οὐ μέντοι οἶμαι ἥξειν αὐτὸ τήμερον.
44a ΚΡ. πόθεν τοῦτο τεκμαίρῃ;
ΣΩ. ἐγώ σοι ἐρῶ· τῇ γάρ που ὑστεραίᾳ δεῖ με
ἀποθνήσκειν ἢ ᾗ ἂν ἔλθῃ τὸ πλοῖον.
ΚΡ. φασί γέ τοι δὴ οἱ τούτων κύριοι.
a5 ΣΩ. οὐ τοίνυν τῆς ἐπιούσης ἡμέρας οἶμαι αὐτὸ ἥξειν
ἀλλὰ τῆς ἑτέρας. τεκμαίρομαι δὲ ἔκ τινος ἐνυπνίου ὃ
ἑώρακα ὀλίγον πρότερον ταύτης τῆς νυκτός· καὶ κινδυνεύεις ἐν καιρῷ τινι οὐκ ἐγεῖραί με.
ΚΡ. ἦν δὲ δὴ τί τὸ ἐνύπνιον;
a10 ΣΩ. ἐδόκει τίς μοι γυνὴ προσελθοῦσα καλὴ καὶ
44b εὐειδής, λευκὰ ἱμάτια ἔχουσα, καλέσαι με καὶ εἰπεῖν· " ὦ
Σώκρατες,
ἤματί κεν τριτάτῳ Φθίην ἐρίβωλον ἵκοιο."
ΚΡ. ὡς ἄτοπον τὸ ἐνύπνιον, ὦ Σώκρατες.
b5 ΣΩ. ἐναργὲς μὲν οὖν, ὥς γέ μοι δοκεῖ, ὦ Κρίτων.
ΚΡ. λίαν γε, ὡς ἔοικεν. ἀλλ᾽, ὦ δαιμόνιε Σώκρατες, ἔτι
καὶ νῦν ἐμοὶ πιθοῦ καὶ σώθητι· ὡς ἐμοί, ἐὰν σὺ ἀποθάνῃς,
οὐ μία συμφορά ἐστιν, ἀλλὰ χωρὶς μὲν τοῦ ἐστερῆσθαι
τοιούτου ἐπιτηδείου οἷον ἐγὼ οὐδένα μή ποτε εὑρήσω, ἔτι
b10 δὲ καὶ πολλοῖς δόξω, οἳ ἐμὲ καὶ σὲ μὴ σαφῶς ἴσασιν, ὡς
44c οἷός τ᾽ ὢν σε σῴζειν εἰ ἤθελον ἀναλίσκειν χρήματα,
ἀμελῆσαι. καίτοι τίς ἂν αἰσχίων εἴη ταύτης δόξα ἢ δοκεῖν
χρήματα περὶ πλείονος ποιεῖσθαι ἢ φίλους; οὐ γὰρ
πείσονται οἱ πολλοὶ ὡς σὺ αὐτὸς οὐκ ἠθέλησας ἀπιέναι
c5 ἐνθένδε ἡμῶν προθυμουμένων.
ΣΩ. ἀλλὰ τί ἡμῖν, ὦ μακάριε Κρίτων, οὕτω τῆς τῶν
πολλῶν δόξης μέλει; οἱ γὰρ ἐπιεικέστατοι, ὧν μᾶλλον
ἄξιον φροντίζειν, ἡγήσονται αὐτὰ οὕτω πεπρᾶχθαι ὥσπερ
ἂν πραχθῇ.
44d ΚΡ. ἀλλ᾽ ὁρᾷς δὴ ὅτι ἀνάγκη, ὦ Σώκρατες, καὶ τῆς
τῶν πολλῶν δόξης μέλειν. αὐτὰ δὲ δῆλα τὰ παρόντα νυνὶ
ὅτι οἷοί τ᾽ εἰσὶν οἱ πολλοὶ οὐ τὰ σμικρότατα τῶν κακῶν
ἐξεργάζεσθαι ἀλλὰ τὰ μέγιστα σχεδόν, ἐάν τις ἐν αὐτοῖς
d5 διαβεβλημένος ᾖ.
ΣΩ. εἰ γὰρ ὤφελον, ὦ Κρίτων, οἷοί τ᾽ εἶναι οἱ πολλοὶ
τὰ μέγιστα κακὰ ἐργάζεσθαι, ἵνα οἷοί τ᾽ ἦσαν καὶ ἀγαθὰ τὰ

μέγιστα, καὶ καλῶς ἂν εἶχεν. νῦν δὲ οὐδέτερα οἷοί τε· οὔτε
γὰρ φρόνιμον οὔτε ἄφρονα δυνατοὶ ποιῆσαι, ποιοῦσι δὲ
d10 τοῦτο ὅτι ἂν τύχωσι.
44e ΚΡ. ταῦτα μὲν δὴ οὕτως ἐχέτω· τάδε δέ, ὦ Σώκρατες,
εἰπέ μοι. ἀρά γε μὴ ἐμοῦ προμηθῇ καὶ τῶν ἄλλων ἐπιτηδείων μή, ἐὰν σὺ ἐνθένδε ἐξέλθῃς, οἱ συκοφάνται ἡμῖν
πράγματα παρέχωσιν ὡς σὲ ἐνθένδε ἐκκλέψασιν, καὶ
e5 ἀναγκασθῶμεν ἢ καὶ πᾶσαν τὴν οὐσίαν ἀποβαλεῖν ἢ συχνὰ
χρήματα, ἢ καὶ ἄλλο τι πρὸς τούτοις παθεῖν; εἰ γάρ τι
45a τοιοῦτον φοβῇ, ἔασον αὐτὸ χαίρειν· ἡμεῖς γάρ που δίκαιοί
ἐσμεν σώσαντές σε κινδυνεύειν τοῦτον τὸν κίνδυνον καὶ ἐὰν
δέῃ ἔτι τούτου μείζω. ἀλλ᾽ ἐμοὶ πείθου καὶ μὴ ἄλλως ποίει.
ΣΩ. καὶ ταῦτα προμηθοῦμαι, ὦ Κρίτων, καὶ ἄλλα
a5 πολλά.
ΚΡ. μήτε τοίνυν ταῦτα φοβοῦ — καὶ γὰρ οὐδὲ πολὺ
τἀργύριόν ἐστιν ὃ θέλουσι λαβόντες τινὲς σῶσαί σε καὶ
ἐξαγαγεῖν ἐνθένδε. ἔπειτα οὐχ ὁρᾷς τούτους τοὺς συκο-
φάντας ὡς εὐτελεῖς, καὶ οὐδὲν ἂν δέοι ἐπ᾽ αὐτοὺς πολλοῦ
45b ἀργυρίου; σοὶ δὲ ὑπάρχει μὲν τὰ ἐμὰ χρήματα, ὡς ἐγὼ
οἶμαι, ἱκανά· ἔπειτα καὶ εἴ τι ἐμοῦ κηδόμενος οὐκ οἴει δεῖν
ἀναλίσκειν τἀμά, ξένοι οὗτοι ἐνθάδε ἕτοιμοι ἀναλίσκειν·
εἷς δὲ καὶ κεκόμικεν ἐπ᾽ αὐτὸ τοῦτο ἀργύριον ἱκανόν, Σιμ-
b5 μίας ὁ Θηβαῖος· ἕτοιμος δὲ καὶ Κέβης καὶ ἄλλοι πολλοὶ
πάνυ. ὥστε, ὅπερ λέγω, μήτε ταῦτα φοβούμενος ἀποκάμῃς σαυτὸν σῶσαι, μήτε, ὃ ἔλεγες ἐν τῷ δικαστηρίῳ,
δυσχερές σοι γενέσθω ὅτι οὐκ ἂν ἔχοις ἐξελθὼν ὅτι χρῷο
45c σαυτῷ· πολλαχοῦ μὲν γὰρ καὶ ἄλλοσε ὅποι ἂν ἀφίκῃ
ἀγαπήσουσί σε· ἐὰν δὲ βούλῃ εἰς Θετταλίαν ἰέναι, εἰσὶν
ἐμοὶ ἐκεῖ ξένοι οἵ σε περὶ πολλοῦ ποιήσονται καὶ ἀσφά-
λειάν σοι παρέξονται, ὥστε σε μηδένα λυπεῖν τῶν κατὰ
c5 Θετταλίαν.
ἔτι δέ, ὦ Σώκρατες, οὐδὲ δίκαιόν μοι δοκεῖς ἐπιχειρεῖν
πρᾶγμα, σαυτὸν προδοῦναι, ἐξὸν σωθῆναι, καὶ τοιαῦτα
σπεύδεις περὶ σαυτὸν γενέσθαι ἅπερ ἂν καὶ οἱ ἐχθροί σου
σπεύσαιέν τε καὶ ἔσπευσαν σὲ διαφθεῖραι βουλόμενοι.
c10 πρὸς δὲ τούτοις καὶ τοὺς ὑεῖς τοὺς σαυτοῦ ἔμοιγε δοκεῖς
45d προδιδόναι, οὕς σοι ἐξὸν καὶ ἐκθρέψαι καὶ ἐκπαιδεῦσαι
οἰχήσῃ καταλιπών, καὶ τὸ σὸν μέρος ὅτι ἂν τύχωσι τοῦτο
πράξουσιν· τεύξονται δέ, ὡς τὸ εἰκός, τοιούτων οἷάπερ
εἴωθεν γίγνεσθαι ἐν ταῖς ὀρφανίαις περὶ τοὺς ὀρφανούς. ἢ
d5 γὰρ οὐ χρὴ ποιεῖσθαι παῖδας ἢ συνδιαταλαιπωρεῖν καὶ

3

ΠΛΑΤΩΝΟΣ

τρέφοντα καὶ παιδεύοντα· σὺ δέ μοι δοκεῖς τὰ ῥᾳθυμότατα
αἱρεῖσθαι. χρὴ δέ, ἅπερ ἂν ἀνὴρ ἀγαθὸς καὶ ἀνδρεῖος
ἕλοιτο, ταῦτα αἱρεῖσθαι, φάσκοντά γε δὴ ἀρετῆς διὰ
παντὸς τοῦ βίου ἐπιμελεῖσθαι· ὡς ἔγωγε καὶ ὑπὲρ σοῦ καὶ
45e ὑπὲρ ἡμῶν τῶν σῶν ἐπιτηδείων αἰσχύνομαι μὴ δόξῃ ἅπαν
τὸ πρᾶγμα τὸ περὶ σὲ ἀνανδρίᾳ τινὶ τῇ ἡμετέρᾳ πεπρᾶχθαι,
καὶ ἡ εἴσοδος τῆς δίκης εἰς τὸ δικαστήριον ὡς εἰσῆλθεν
ἐξὸν μὴ εἰσελθεῖν, καὶ αὐτὸς ὁ ἀγὼν τῆς δίκης ὡς ἐγένετο,
e5 καὶ τὸ τελευταῖον δὴ τουτί, ὥσπερ κατάγελως τῆς
πράξεως, κακίᾳ τινὶ καὶ ἀνανδρίᾳ τῇ ἡμετέρᾳ διαπεφευ-
46a γέναι ἡμᾶς δοκεῖν, οἵτινές σε οὐχὶ ἐσώσαμεν οὐδὲ σὺ
σαυτόν, οἷόν τε ὂν καὶ δυνατὸν εἴ τι καὶ σμικρὸν ἡμῶν ὄφελος ἦν. ταῦτα οὖν, ὦ Σώκρατες, ὅρα μὴ ἅμα τῷ κακῷ καὶ
αἰσχρὰ ᾖ σοί τε καὶ ἡμῖν. ἀλλὰ βουλεύου — μᾶλλον δὲ οὐδὲ
a5 βουλεύεσθαι ἔτι ὥρα ἀλλὰ βεβουλεῦσθαι — μία δὲ βουλή·
τῆς γὰρ ἐπιούσης νυκτὸς πάντα ταῦτα δεῖ πεπρᾶχθαι· εἰ δ᾽
ἔτι περιμενοῦμεν, ἀδύνατον καὶ οὐκέτι οἷόν τε. ἀλλὰ παντὶ
τρόπῳ, ὦ Σώκρατες, πείθου μοι καὶ μηδαμῶς ἄλλως
ποίει.
46b ΣΩ. ὦ φίλε Κρίτων, ἡ προθυμία σου πολλοῦ ἀξία εἰ
μετά τινος ὀρθότητος εἴη· εἰ δὲ μή, ὅσῳ μείζων τοσούτῳ
χαλεπωτέρα. σκοπεῖσθαι οὖν χρὴ ἡμᾶς εἴτε ταῦτα
πρακτέον εἴτε μή· ὡς ἐγὼ οὐ νῦν πρῶτον ἀλλὰ καὶ ἀεὶ
b5 τοιοῦτος οἷος τῶν ἐμῶν μηδενὶ ἄλλῳ πείθεσθαι ἢ τῷ λόγῳ
ὃς ἄν μοι λογιζομένῳ βέλτιστος φαίνηται. τοὺς δὴ λόγους
οὓς ἐν τῷ ἔμπροσθεν ἔλεγον οὐ δύναμαι νῦν ἐκβαλεῖν,
ἐπειδή μοι ἥδε ἡ τύχη γέγονεν, ἀλλὰ σχεδόν τι ὅμοιοι
46c φαίνονταί μοι, καὶ τοὺς αὐτοὺς πρεσβεύω καὶ τιμῶ οὕσπερ
καὶ πρότερον· ὧν ἐὰν μὴ βελτίω ἔχωμεν λέγειν ἐν τῷ
παρόντι, εὖ ἴσθι ὅτι οὐ μή σοι συγχωρήσω, οὐδ᾽ ἂν πλείω
τῶν νῦν παρόντων ἡ τῶν πολλῶν δύναμις ὥσπερ παῖδας
c5 ἡμᾶς μορμολύττηται, δεσμοὺς καὶ θανάτους ἐπιπέμπουσα
καὶ χρημάτων ἀφαιρέσεις. πῶς οὖν ἂν μετριώτατα
σκοποίμεθα αὐτά; εἰ πρῶτον μὲν τοῦτον τὸν λόγον ἀναλά-
βοιμεν, ὃν σὺ λέγεις περὶ τῶν δοξῶν. πότερον καλῶς
46d ἐλέγετο ἑκάστοτε ἢ οὔ, ὅτι ταῖς μὲν δεῖ τῶν δοξῶν προσέ-
χειν τὸν νοῦν, ταῖς δὲ οὔ; ἢ πρὶν μὲν ἐμὲ δεῖν ἀποθνῄσκειν
καλῶς ἐλέγετο, νῦν δὲ κατάδηλος ἄρα ἐγένετο ὅτι ἄλλως
ἕνεκα λόγου ἐλέγετο, ἦν δὲ παιδιὰ καὶ φλυαρία ὡς
d5 ἀληθῶς; ἐπιθυμῶ δ᾽ ἔγωγ᾽ ἐπισκέψασθαι, ὦ Κρίτων, κοινῇ
μετὰ σοῦ εἴ τί μοι ἀλλοιότερος φανεῖται, ἐπειδὴ ὧδε ἔχω,

4

ΚΡΙΤΩΝ

ἢ ὁ αὐτός, καὶ ἐάσομεν χαίρειν ἢ πεισόμεθα αὐτῷ. ἐλέγετο
δέ πως, ὡς ἐγῷμαι, ἑκάστοτε ὧδε ὑπὸ τῶν οἰομένων τὶ
λέγειν, ὥσπερ νυνδὴ ἐγὼ ἔλεγον, ὅτι τῶν δοξῶν ἃς οἱ

46e ἄνθρωποι δοξάζουσιν δέοι τὰς μὲν περὶ πολλοῦ ποιεῖσθαι,
τὰς δὲ μή. τοῦτο πρὸς θεῶν, ὦ Κρίτων, οὐ δοκεῖ καλῶς σοι
λέγεσθαι; σὺ γάρ, ὅσα γε τἀνθρώπεια, ἐκτὸς εἶ τοῦ μέλλειν

47a ἀποθνῄσκειν αὔριον, καὶ οὐκ ἂν σὲ παρακρούοι ἡ παροῦσα
συμφορά· σκόπει δή· οὐχ ἱκανῶς δοκεῖ σοι λέγεσθαι ὅτι οὐ
πάσας χρὴ τὰς δόξας τῶν ἀνθρώπων τιμᾶν ἀλλὰ τὰς μέν,
τὰς δ' οὔ, οὐδὲ πάντων ἀλλὰ τῶν μέν, τῶν δ' οὔ; τί φῄς;

a5 ταῦτα οὐχὶ καλῶς λέγεται;
ΚΡ. καλῶς.
ΣΩ. οὐκοῦν τὰς μὲν χρηστὰς τιμᾶν, τὰς δὲ πονηρὰς μή;
ΚΡ. ναί.
ΣΩ. χρησταὶ δὲ οὐχ αἱ τῶν φρονίμων, πονηραὶ δὲ αἱ

a10 τῶν ἀφρόνων;
ΚΡ. πῶς δ' οὔ;
ΣΩ. φέρε δή, πῶς αὖ τὰ τοιαῦτα ἐλέγετο; γυμναζό-

47b μενος ἀνὴρ καὶ τοῦτο πράττων πότερον παντὸς ἀνδρὸς
ἐπαίνῳ καὶ ψόγῳ καὶ δόξῃ τὸν νοῦν προσέχει, ἢ ἑνὸς μόνου
ἐκείνου ὃς ἂν τυγχάνῃ ἰατρὸς ἢ παιδοτρίβης ὤν;
ΚΡ. ἑνὸς μόνου.

b5 ΣΩ. οὐκοῦν φοβεῖσθαι χρὴ τοὺς ψόγους καὶ ἀσπά-
ζεσθαι τοὺς ἐπαίνους τοὺς τοῦ ἑνὸς ἐκείνου ἀλλὰ μὴ τοὺς
τῶν πολλῶν.
ΚΡ. δῆλα δή.
ΣΩ. ταύτῃ ἄρα αὐτῷ πρακτέον καὶ γυμναστέον καὶ

b10 ἐδεστέον γε καὶ ποτέον, ᾗ ἂν τῷ ἑνὶ δοκῇ, τῷ ἐπιστάτῃ καὶ
ἐπαΐοντι, μᾶλλον ἢ ᾗ σύμπασι τοῖς ἄλλοις.
ΚΡ. ἔστι ταῦτα.

47c ΣΩ. εἶεν. ἀπειθήσας δὲ τῷ ἑνὶ καὶ ἀτιμάσας αὐτοῦ τὴν
δόξαν καὶ τοὺς ἐπαίνους, τιμήσας δὲ τοὺς τῶν πολλῶν καὶ
μηδὲν ἐπαϊόντων, ἆρα οὐδὲν κακὸν πείσεται;
ΚΡ. πῶς γὰρ οὔ;

c5 ΣΩ. τί δ' ἔστι τὸ κακὸν τοῦτο, καὶ ποῖ τείνει, καὶ εἰς τί
τῶν τοῦ ἀπειθοῦντος;
ΚΡ. δῆλον ὅτι εἰς τὸ σῶμα· τοῦτο γὰρ διόλλυσι.
ΣΩ. καλῶς λέγεις. οὐκοῦν καὶ τἆλλα, ὦ Κρίτων,
οὕτως, ἵνα μὴ πάντα διΐωμεν, καὶ δὴ καὶ περὶ τῶν δικαίων

c10 καὶ ἀδίκων καὶ αἰσχρῶν καὶ καλῶν καὶ ἀγαθῶν καὶ
κακῶν, περὶ ὧν νῦν ἡ βουλὴ ἡμῖν ἐστιν; πότερον τῇ τῶν

5

47d πολλῶν δόξῃ δεῖ ἡμᾶς ἕπεσθαι καὶ φοβεῖσθαι αὐτὴν ἢ τῇ
τοῦ ἑνός, εἴ τίς ἐστιν ἐπαΐων, ὃν δεῖ καὶ αἰσχύνεσθαι καὶ
φοβεῖσθαι μᾶλλον ἢ σύμπαντας τοὺς ἄλλους; ᾧ εἰ μὴ
ἀκολουθήσομεν, διαφθεροῦμεν ἐκεῖνο καὶ λωβησόμεθα, ὃ
d5 τῷ μὲν δικαίῳ βέλτιον ἐγίγνετο, τῷ δὲ ἀδίκῳ ἀπώλλυτο. ἢ
οὐδέν ἐστι τοῦτο;
ΚΡ. οἶμαι ἔγωγε, ὦ Σώκρατες.
ΣΩ. φέρε δή, ἐὰν τὸ ὑπὸ τοῦ ὑγιεινοῦ μὲν βέλτιον
γιγνόμενον, ὑπὸ τοῦ νοσώδους δὲ διαφθειρόμενον
d10 διολέσωμεν πειθόμενοι μὴ τῇ τῶν ἐπαϊόντων δόξῃ, ἆρα
47e βιωτὸν ἡμῖν ἐστιν διεφθαρμένου αὐτοῦ; ἔστι δέ που τοῦτο
σῶμα· ἢ οὐχί;
ΚΡ. ναί.
ΣΩ. ἆρ᾽ οὖν βιωτὸν ἡμῖν ἐστιν μετὰ μοχθηροῦ καὶ
e5 διεφθαρμένου σώματος;
ΚΡ. οὐδαμῶς.
ΣΩ. ἀλλὰ μετ᾽ ἐκείνου ἆρ᾽ ἡμῖν βιωτὸν διεφθαρμένου,
ὃ τὸ ἄδικον μὲν λωβᾶται, τὸ δὲ δίκαιον ὀνίνησιν; ἢ φαυλό-
τερον ἡγούμεθα εἶναι τοῦ σώματος ἐκεῖνο, ὅτι ποτ᾽ ἐστὶ
48a τῶν ἡμετέρων, περὶ ὃ ἥ τε ἀδικία καὶ ἡ δικαιοσύνη ἐστίν;
ΚΡ. οὐδαμῶς.
ΣΩ. ἀλλὰ τιμιώτερον;
ΚΡ. πολύ γε.
a5 ΣΩ. οὐκ ἄρα, ὦ βέλτιστε, πάνυ ἡμῖν οὕτω φροντιστέον
τί ἐροῦσιν οἱ πολλοὶ ἡμᾶς, ἀλλ᾽ ὅτι ὁ ἐπαΐων περὶ τῶν
δικαίων καὶ ἀδίκων, ὁ εἷς, καὶ αὐτὴ ἡ ἀλήθεια. ὥστε
πρῶτον μὲν ταύτῃ οὐκ ὀρθῶς εἰσηγῇ, εἰσηγούμενος τῆς
τῶν πολλῶν δόξης δεῖν ἡμᾶς φροντίζειν περὶ τῶν δικαίων
a10 καὶ καλῶν καὶ ἀγαθῶν καὶ τῶν ἐναντίων. "ἀλλὰ μὲν δή,"
φαίη γ᾽ ἄν τις, "οἷοί τέ εἰσιν ἡμᾶς οἱ πολλοὶ ἀποκτεινύναι."
48b ΚΡ. δῆλα δὴ καὶ ταῦτα· φαίη γὰρ ἄν, ὦ Σώκρατες.
ΣΩ. ἀληθῆ λέγεις. ἀλλ᾽, ὦ θαυμάσιε, οὗτός τε ὁ λόγος
ὃν διεληλύθαμεν ἔμοιγε δοκεῖ ἔτι ὅμοιος εἶναι καὶ
πρότερον· καὶ τόνδε δὲ αὖ σκόπει εἰ ἔτι μένει ἡμῖν ἢ οὔ, ὅτι
b5 οὐ τὸ ζῆν περὶ πλείστου ποιητέον, ἀλλὰ τὸ εὖ ζῆν.
ΚΡ. ἀλλὰ μένει.
ΣΩ. τὸ δὲ εὖ καὶ καλῶς καὶ δικαίως ὅτι ταὐτόν ἐστιν,
μένει ἢ οὐ μένει;
ΚΡ. μένει.
b10 ΣΩ. οὐκοῦν ἐκ τῶν ὁμολογουμένων τοῦτο σκεπτέον,
πότερον δίκαιον ἐμὲ ἐνθένδε πειρᾶσθαι ἐξιέναι μὴ

48c ἀφιέντων Ἀθηναίων ἢ οὐ δίκαιον· καὶ ἐὰν μὲν φαίνηται
δίκαιον, πειρώμεθα, εἰ δὲ μή, ἐῶμεν. ἃς δὲ σὺ λέγεις τὰς
σκέψεις περὶ τε ἀναλώσεως χρημάτων καὶ δόξης καὶ
παίδων τροφῆς, μὴ ὡς ἀληθῶς ταῦτα, ὦ Κρίτων, σκέμ-
c5 ματα ᾖ τῶν ῥᾳδίως ἀποκτεινύντων καὶ ἀναβιωσκομένων
γ᾽ ἄν, εἰ οἷοί τ᾽ ἦσαν, οὐδενὶ ξὺν νῷ, τούτων τῶν πολλῶν.
ἡμῖν δ᾽, ἐπειδὴ ὁ λόγος οὕτως αἱρεῖ, μὴ οὐδὲν ἄλλο
σκεπτέον ᾖ ἢ ὅπερ νυνδὴ ἐλέγομεν, πότερον δίκαια πράξο-
μεν καὶ χρήματα τελοῦντες τούτοις τοῖς ἐμὲ ἐνθένδε
48d ἐξάξουσιν καὶ χάριτας, καὶ αὐτοὶ ἐξάγοντές τε καὶ
ἐξαγόμενοι, ἢ τῇ ἀληθείᾳ ἀδικήσομεν πάντα ταῦτα
ποιοῦντες· κἂν φαινώμεθα ἄδικα αὐτὰ ἐργαζόμενοι, μὴ οὐ
δέῃ ὑπολογίζεσθαι οὔτ᾽ εἰ ἀποθνῄσκειν δεῖ παραμένοντας
d5 καὶ ἡσυχίαν ἄγοντας, οὔτε ἄλλο ὁτιοῦν πάσχειν πρὸ τοῦ
ἀδικεῖν.
ΚΡ. καλῶς μέν μοι δοκεῖς λέγειν, ὦ Σώκρατες· ὅρα δὲ
τί δρῶμεν.
ΣΩ. σκοπῶμεν, ὦ ἀγαθέ, κοινῇ, καὶ εἴ πη ἔχεις ἀντι-
48e λέγειν ἐμοῦ λέγοντος, ἀντίλεγε, καί σοι πείσομαι· εἰ δὲ μή,
παῦσαι ἤδη, ὦ μακάριε, πολλάκις μοι λέγων τὸν αὐτὸν
λόγον, ὡς χρὴ ἐνθένδε ἀκόντων Ἀθηναίων ἐμὲ ἀπιέναι· ὡς
ἐγὼ περὶ πολλοῦ ποιοῦμαι πείσας σε ταῦτα πράττειν, ἀλλὰ
e5 μὴ ἄκοντος. ὅρα δὲ δὴ τῆς σκέψεως τὴν ἀρχὴν ἐάν σοι
49a ἱκανῶς λέγηται, καὶ πειρῶ ἀποκρίνεσθαι τὸ ἐρωτώμενον ᾗ
ἂν μάλιστα οἴῃ.
ΚΡ. ἀλλὰ πειράσομαι.
ΣΩ. οὐδενὶ τρόπῳ φαμὲν ἑκόντας ἀδικητέον εἶναι, ἢ
a5 τινὶ μὲν ἀδικητέον τρόπῳ τινὶ δὲ οὔ; ἢ οὐδαμῶς τό γε
ἀδικεῖν οὔτε ἀγαθὸν οὔτε καλόν, ὡς πολλάκις ἡμῖν καὶ ἐν
τῷ ἔμπροσθεν χρόνῳ ὡμολογήθη;* ἢ πᾶσαι ἡμῖν ἐκεῖναι αἱ
πρόσθεν ὁμολογίαι ἐν ταῖσδε ταῖς ὀλίγαις ἡμέραις ἐκκεχυμέναι εἰσίν, καὶ πάλαι, ὦ Κρίτων, ἄρα τηλικοίδε** ἄνδρες
a10 πρὸς ἀλλήλους σπουδῇ διαλεγόμενοι ἐλάθομεν ἡμᾶς
49b αὐτοὺς παίδων οὐδὲν διαφέροντες; ἢ παντὸς μᾶλλον οὕτως
ἔχει ὥσπερ τότε ἐλέγετο ἡμῖν· εἴτε φασὶν οἱ πολλοὶ εἴτε μή,
καὶ εἴτε δεῖ ἡμᾶς ἔτι τῶνδε χαλεπώτερα πάσχειν εἴτε καὶ
πρᾳότερα, ὅμως τό γε ἀδικεῖν τῷ ἀδικοῦντι καὶ κακὸν καὶ
b5 αἰσχρὸν τυγχάνει ὂν παντὶ τρόπῳ; φαμὲν ἢ οὔ;

* Most witnesses to the text insert here the words ὅπερ καὶ ἄρτι ἐλέγετο.

** Another insertion here, or after ἄνδρες (all witnesses): γέροντες.

ΚΡ. φαμέν.

ΣΩ. οὐδαμῶς ἄρα δεῖ ἀδικεῖν.

ΚΡ. οὐ δῆτα.

ΣΩ. οὐδὲ ἀδικούμενον ἄρα ἀνταδικεῖν, ὡς οἱ πολλοὶ

b10 οἴονται, ἐπειδή γε οὐδαμῶς δεῖ ἀδικεῖν.

49c ΚΡ. οὐ φαίνεται.

ΣΩ. τί δὲ δή; κακουργεῖν δεῖ, ὦ Κρίτων, ἢ οὔ;

ΚΡ. οὐ δεῖ δήπου, ὦ Σώκρατες.

ΣΩ. τί δέ; ἀντικακουργεῖν κακῶς πάσχοντα, ὡς οἱ

c5 πολλοί φασιν, δίκαιον ἢ οὐ δίκαιον;

ΚΡ. οὐδαμῶς.

ΣΩ. τὸ γάρ που κακῶς ποιεῖν ἀνθρώπους τοῦ ἀδικεῖν

οὐδὲν διαφέρει.

ΚΡ. ἀληθῆ λέγεις.

c10 ΣΩ. οὔτε ἄρα ἀνταδικεῖν δεῖ οὔτε κακῶς ποιεῖν οὐδένα

ἀνθρώπων, οὐδ᾽ ἂν ὁτιοῦν πάσχῃ ὑπ᾽ αὐτῶν. καὶ ὅρα, ὦ

49d Κρίτων, ταῦτα καθομολογῶν, ὅπως μὴ παρὰ δόξαν ὁμο-

λογῇς· οἶδα γὰρ ὅτι ὀλίγοις τισὶ ταῦτα καὶ δοκεῖ καὶ δόξει.

οἷς οὖν οὕτω δέδοκται καὶ οἷς μή, τούτοις οὐκ ἔστι κοινὴ

βουλή, ἀλλὰ ἀνάγκη τούτους ἀλλήλων καταφρονεῖν

d5 ὁρῶντας τὰ ἀλλήλων βουλεύματα. σκόπει δὴ οὖν καὶ σὺ εὖ

μάλα πότερον κοινωνεῖς καὶ συνδοκεῖ σοι καὶ ἀρχώμεθα

ἐντεῦθεν βουλευόμενοι, ὡς οὐδέποτε ὀρθῶς ἔχοντος οὔτε

τοῦ ἀδικεῖν οὔτε τοῦ ἀνταδικεῖν οὔτε κακῶς πάσχοντα

ἀμύνεσθαι ἀντιδρῶντα κακῶς, ἢ ἀφίστασαι καὶ οὐ κοινω-

49e νεῖς τῆς ἀρχῆς; ἐμοὶ μὲν γὰρ καὶ πάλαι οὕτω καὶ νῦν ἔτι

δοκεῖ, σοὶ δὲ εἴ πῃ ἄλλῃ δέδοκται, λέγε καὶ δίδασκε. εἰ δ᾽

ἐμμένεις τοῖς πρόσθε, τὸ μετὰ τοῦτο ἄκουε.

ΚΡ. ἀλλ᾽ ἐμμένω τε καὶ συνδοκεῖ μοι· ἀλλὰ λέγε.

e5 ΣΩ. λέγω δὴ αὖ τὸ μετὰ τοῦτο, μᾶλλον δ᾽ ἐρωτῶ·

πότερον ἃ ἄν τις ὁμολογήσῃ τῳ δίκαια ὄντα ποιητέον ἢ

ἐξαπατητέον;

ΚΡ. ποιητέον.

ΣΩ. ἐκ τούτων δὴ ἄθρει. ἀπιόντες ἐνθένδε ἡμεῖς μὴ

50a πείσαντες τὴν πόλιν πότερον κακῶς τινας ποιοῦμεν, καὶ

ταῦτα οὓς ἥκιστα δεῖ, ἢ οὔ; καὶ ἐμμένομεν οἷς ὡμολογή-

σαμεν δικαίοις οὖσιν ἢ οὔ;

ΚΡ. οὐκ ἔχω, ὦ Σώκρατες, ἀποκρίνασθαι πρὸς ὃ

a5 ἐρωτᾷς· οὐ γὰρ ἐννοῶ.

ΣΩ. ἀλλ᾽ ὧδε σκόπει. εἰ μέλλουσιν ἡμῖν ἐνθένδε εἴτε

ἀποδιδράσκειν, εἴθ᾽ ὅπως δεῖ ὀνομάσαι τοῦτο, ἐλθόντες οἱ

ΚΡΙΤΩΝ

νόμοι καὶ τὸ κοινὸν τῆς πόλεως ἐπιστάντες ἔροιντο· "εἰπέ
μοι, ὦ Σώκρατες, τί ἐν νῷ ἔχεις ποιεῖν; ἄλλο τι ἢ τούτῳ τῷ
50b ἔργῳ ᾧ ἐπιχειρεῖς διανοῇ τούς τε νόμους ἡμᾶς ἀπολέσαι
καὶ σύμπασαν τὴν πόλιν τὸ σὸν μέρος; ἢ δοκεῖ σοι οἷόν τε
ἔτι ἐκείνην τὴν πόλιν εἶναι καὶ μὴ ἀνατετράφθαι, ἐν ᾗ ἂν αἱ
γενόμεναι δίκαι μηδὲν ἰσχύωσιν ἀλλὰ ὑπὸ ἰδιωτῶν ἄκυροί
b5 τε γίγνωνται καὶ διαφθείρωνται;" τί ἐροῦμεν, ὦ Κρίτων,
πρὸς ταῦτα καὶ ἄλλα τοιαῦτα; πολλὰ γὰρ ἄν τις ἔχοι,
ἄλλως τε καὶ ῥήτωρ, εἰπεῖν ὑπὲρ τούτου τοῦ νόμου ἀπολλυμένου ὃς τὰς δίκας τὰς δικασθείσας προστάττει κυρίας
50c εἶναι. ἢ ἐροῦμεν πρὸς αὐτοὺς ὅτι "ἠδίκει γὰρ ἡμᾶς ἡ
πόλις καὶ οὐκ ὀρθῶς τὴν δίκην ἔκρινεν;" ταῦτα ἢ τί
ἐροῦμεν;
ΚΡ. ταῦτα νὴ Δία, ὦ Σώκρατες.
c5 ΣΩ. τί οὖν ἂν εἴπωσιν οἱ νόμοι· "ὦ Σώκρατες, ἢ καὶ
ταῦτα ὡμολόγητο ἡμῖν τε καὶ σοί, ἢ ἐμμενεῖν ταῖς δίκαις
αἷς ἂν ἡ πόλις δικάζῃ;" εἰ οὖν αὐτῶν θαυμάζοιμεν
λεγόντων, ἴσως ἂν εἴποιεν ὅτι "ὦ Σώκρατες, μὴ θαύμαζε
τὰ λεγόμενα, ἀλλ᾽ ἀποκρίνου, ἐπειδὴ καὶ εἴωθας χρῆσθαι
c10 τῷ ἐρωτᾶν τε καὶ ἀποκρίνεσθαι. φέρε γάρ, τί ἐγκαλῶν
50d ἡμῖν καὶ τῇ πόλει ἐπιχειρεῖς ἡμᾶς ἀπολλύναι; οὐ πρῶτον
μέν σε ἐγεννήσαμεν ἡμεῖς, καὶ δι᾽ ἡμῶν ἔλαβε τὴν μητέρα
σου ὁ πατὴρ καὶ ἐφύτευσέν σε; φράσον οὖν, τούτοις ἡμῶν,
τοῖς νόμοις τοῖς περὶ τοὺς γάμους, μέμφῃ τι ὡς οὐ καλῶς
d5 ἔχουσιν; "οὐ μέμφομαι," φαίην ἄν. "ἀλλὰ τοῖς περὶ τὴν
τοῦ γενομένου τροφήν τε καὶ παιδείαν ἐν ᾗ καὶ σὺ ἐπαιδεύθης; ἢ οὐ καλῶς προσέταττον ἡμῶν οἱ ἐπὶ τούτῳ τεταγμένοι νόμοι, παραγγέλλοντες τῷ πατρὶ τῷ σῷ σε ἐν μουσικῇ
50e καὶ γυμναστικῇ παιδεύειν;" "καλῶς," φαίην ἄν. "εἶεν.
ἐπειδὴ δὲ ἐγένου τε καὶ ἐξετράφης καὶ ἐπαιδεύθης, ἔχοις
ἂν εἰπεῖν πρῶτον μὲν ὡς οὐχὶ ἡμέτερος ἦσθα καὶ ἔκγονος
καὶ δοῦλος, αὐτός τε καὶ οἱ σοὶ πρόγονοι; καὶ εἰ τοῦθ᾽
e5 οὕτως ἔχει, ἆρ᾽ ἐξ ἴσου οἴει εἶναι σοὶ τὸ δίκαιον καὶ ἡμῖν,
καὶ ἅττ᾽ ἂν ἡμεῖς σε ἐπιχειρῶμεν ποιεῖν, καὶ σοὶ ταῦτα
ἀντιποιεῖν οἴει δίκαιον εἶναι; ἢ πρὸς μὲν ἄρα σοι τὸν
πατέρα οὐκ ἐξ ἴσου ἦν τὸ δίκαιον καὶ πρὸς δεσπότην, εἴ σοι
ὢν ἐτύγχανεν, ὥστε ἅπερ πάσχοις ταῦτα καὶ ἀντιποιεῖν,
51a οὔτε κακῶς ἀκούοντα ἀντιλέγειν οὔτε τυπτόμενον ἀντιτύπτειν οὔτε ἄλλα τοιαῦτα πολλά· πρὸς δὲ τὴν πατρίδα
ἄρα καὶ τοὺς νόμους ἐξέσται σοι, ὥστε, ἐάν σε ἐπιχειρῶμεν
ἡμεῖς ἀπολλύναι δίκαιον ἡγούμενοι εἶναι, καὶ σὺ δὲ ἡμᾶς

9

ΠΛΑΤΩΝΟΣ

a5 τοὺς νόμους καὶ τὴν πατρίδα καθ' ὅσον δύνασαι ἐπιχειρή-
σεις ἀνταπολλύναι, καὶ φήσεις ταῦτα ποιῶν δίκαια πράττειν, ὁ τῇ ἀληθείᾳ τῆς ἀρετῆς ἐπιμελούμενος; ἢ οὕτως εἶ
σοφὸς ὥστε λέληθέν σε ὅτι μητρός τε καὶ πατρὸς καὶ τῶν
ἄλλων προγόνων ἁπάντων τιμιώτερόν ἐστι πατρὶς καὶ
51b σεμνότερον καὶ ἁγιώτερον καὶ ἐν μείζονι μοίρᾳ καὶ παρὰ
θεοῖς καὶ παρ' ἀνθρώποις τοῖς νοῦν ἔχουσι, καὶ σέβεσθαι
δεῖ καὶ μᾶλλον ὑπείκειν καὶ θωπεύειν πατρίδα χαλεπαίνουσαν ἢ πατέρα, καὶ ἢ πείθειν ἢ ποιεῖν ἃ ἂν κελεύῃ, καὶ
b5 πάσχειν ἐάν τι προστάττῃ παθεῖν ἡσυχίαν ἄγοντα, ἐάντε
τύπτεσθαι ἐάντε δεῖσθαι, ἐάντε εἰς πόλεμον ἄγῃ τρωθησόμενον ἢ ἀποθανούμενον, ποιητέον ταῦτα, καὶ τὸ δίκαιον
οὕτως ἔχει, καὶ οὐχὶ ὑπεικτέον οὐδὲ ἀναχωρητέον οὐδὲ
λειπτέον τὴν τάξιν, ἀλλὰ καὶ ἐν πολέμῳ καὶ ἐν δικαστηρίῳ
b10 καὶ πανταχοῦ ποιητέον ἃ ἂν κελεύῃ ἡ πόλις καὶ ἡ πατρίς, ἢ
51c πείθειν αὐτὴν ᾗ τὸ δίκαιον πέφυκε· βιάζεσθαι δὲ οὐχ ὅσιον
οὔτε μητέρα οὔτε πατέρα, πολὺ δὲ τούτων ἔτι ἧττον τὴν
πατρίδα;" τί φήσομεν πρὸς ταῦτα, ὦ Κρίτων; ἀληθῆ
λέγειν τοὺς νόμους ἢ οὔ;
c5 ΚΡ. ἔμοιγε δοκεῖ.
ΣΩ. "σκόπει τοίνυν, ὦ Σώκρατες," φαῖεν ἂν ἴσως οἱ
νόμοι, "εἰ ἡμεῖς ταῦτα ἀληθῆ λέγομεν, ὅτι οὐ δίκαια ἡμᾶς
ἐπιχειρεῖς δρᾶν ἃ νῦν ἐπιχειρεῖς. ἡμεῖς γάρ σε γεννή-
σαντες, ἐκθρέψαντες, παιδεύσαντες, μεταδόντες ἁπάντων
51d ὧν οἷοί τ' ἦμεν καλῶν σοὶ καὶ τοῖς ἄλλοις πᾶσιν πολίταις,
ὅμως προαγορεύομεν τῷ ἐξουσίαν πεποιηκέναι Ἀθηναίων
τῷ βουλομένῳ, ἐπειδὰν δοκιμασθῇ καὶ ἴδῃ τὰ ἐν τῇ πόλει
πράγματα καὶ ἡμᾶς τοὺς νόμους, ᾧ ἂν μὴ ἀρέσκωμεν
d5 ἡμεῖς ἐξεῖναι λαβόντα τὰ αὑτοῦ ἀπιέναι ὅποι ἂν βούληται.
καὶ οὐδεὶς ἡμῶν τῶν νόμων ἐμποδών ἐστιν οὐδ' ἀπα-
γορεύει, ἐάντε τις βούληται ὑμῶν εἰς ἀποικίαν ἰέναι, εἰ μὴ
ἀρέσκοιμεν ἡμεῖς τε καὶ ἡ πόλις, ἐάντε μετοικεῖν ἄλλοσέ
51e ποι ἐλθών, ἰέναι ἐκεῖσε ὅποι ἂν βούληται ἔχοντα τὰ αὑτοῦ.
ὃς δ' ἂν ὑμῶν παραμείνῃ, ὁρῶν ὃν τρόπον ἡμεῖς τάς τε
δίκας δικάζομεν καὶ τἆλλα τὴν πόλιν διοικοῦμεν, ἤδη
φαμὲν τοῦτον ὡμολογηκέναι ἔργῳ ἡμῖν ἃ ἂν ἡμεῖς
e5 κελεύωμεν ποιήσειν ταῦτα, καὶ τὸν μὴ πειθόμενον τριχῇ
φαμεν ἀδικεῖν, ὅτι τε γεννηταῖς οὖσιν ἡμῖν οὐ πείθεται, καὶ
ὅτι τροφεῦσι, καὶ ὅτι ὁμολογήσας ἡμῖν πείσεσθαι οὔτε πείθεται οὔτε πείθει ἡμᾶς εἰ μὴ καλῶς τι ποιοῦμεν, προτι-
52a θέντων ἡμῶν καὶ οὐκ ἀγρίως ἐπιταττόντων ποιεῖν ἃ ἂν

10

ΚΡΙΤΩΝ

κελεύωμεν, ἀλλὰ ἐφιέντων δυοῖν θάτερα, ἢ πείθειν ἡμᾶς ἢ
ποιεῖν, τούτων οὐδέτερα ποιεῖ. ταύταις δή φαμεν καὶ σέ, ὦ
Σώκρατες, ταῖς αἰτίαις ἐνέξεσθαι, εἴπερ ποιήσεις ἃ ἐπι-
a5 νοεῖς, καὶ οὐχ ἥκιστα Ἀθηναίων σέ, ἀλλ' ἐν τοῖς μάλιστα."
εἰ οὖν ἐγὼ εἴποιμι· "διὰ τί δή;" ἴσως ἄν μου δικαίως
καθάπτοιντο λέγοντες ὅτι ἐν τοῖς μάλιστα Ἀθηναίων ἐγὼ
αὐτοῖς ὡμολογηκὼς τυγχάνω ταύτην τὴν ὁμολογίαν.
52b φαῖεν γὰρ ἂν ὅτι "ὦ Σώκρατες, μεγάλα ἡμῖν τούτων
τεκμήριά ἐστιν, ὅτι σοι καὶ ἡμεῖς ἠρέσκομεν καὶ ἡ πόλις·
οὐ γὰρ ἄν ποτε τῶν ἄλλων Ἀθηναίων ἁπάντων διαφερόντως ἐν αὐτῇ ἐπεδήμεις εἰ μή σοι διαφερόντως
b5 ἤρεσκεν, καὶ οὔτ' ἐπὶ θεωρίαν πώποτ' ἐκ τῆς πόλεως
ἐξῆλθες, ὅτι μὴ ἅπαξ εἰς Ἰσθμόν, οὔτε ἄλλοσε οὐδαμόσε,
εἰ μή ποι στρατευσόμενος, οὔτε ἄλλην ἀποδημίαν ἐποιήσω
πώποτε ὥσπερ οἱ ἄλλοι ἄνθρωποι, οὐδ' ἐπιθυμία σε ἄλλης
πόλεως οὐδὲ ἄλλων νόμων ἔλαβεν εἰδέναι, ἀλλὰ ἡμεῖς σοι
52c ἱκανοὶ ἦμεν καὶ ἡ ἡμετέρα πόλις· οὕτω σφόδρα ἡμᾶς ᾑροῦ
καὶ ὡμολόγεις καθ' ἡμᾶς πολιτεύσεσθαι, τά τε ἄλλα καὶ
παῖδας ἐν αὐτῇ ἐποιήσω, ὡς ἀρεσκούσης σοι τῆς πόλεως.
ἔτι τοίνυν ἐν αὐτῇ τῇ δίκῃ ἐξῆν σοι φυγῆς τιμήσασθαι εἰ
c5 ἐβούλου, καὶ ὅπερ νῦν ἀκούσης τῆς πόλεως ἐπιχειρεῖς,
τότε ἑκούσης ποιῆσαι. σὺ δὲ τότε μὲν ἐκαλλωπίζου ὡς οὐκ
ἀγανακτῶν εἰ δέοι τεθνάναι σε, ἀλλὰ ᾑροῦ, ὡς ἔφησθα,
πρὸ τῆς φυγῆς θάνατον· νῦν δὲ οὔτ' ἐκείνους τοὺς λόγους
αἰσχύνῃ, οὔτε ἡμῶν τῶν νόμων ἐντρέπῃ, ἐπιχειρῶν δια-
52d φθεῖραι, πράττεις τε ἅπερ ἂν δοῦλος ὁ φαυλότατος
πράξειεν, ἀποδιδράσκειν ἐπιχειρῶν παρὰ τὰς συνθήκας τε
καὶ τὰς ὁμολογίας καθ' ἃς ἡμῖν συνέθου πολιτεύεσθαι.
πρῶτον μὲν οὖν ἡμῖν τοῦτ' αὐτὸ ἀπόκριναι, εἰ ἀληθῆ
d5 λέγομεν φάσκοντές σε ὡμολογηκέναι πολιτεύσεσθαι καθ'
ἡμᾶς ἔργῳ ἀλλ' οὐ λόγῳ, ἢ οὐκ ἀληθῆ." τί φῶμεν πρὸς
ταῦτα, ὦ Κρίτων; ἄλλο τι ἢ ὁμολογῶμεν;
ΚΡ. ἀνάγκη, ὦ Σώκρατες.
ΣΩ. "ἄλλο τι οὖν," ἂν φαῖεν, "ἢ συνθήκας τὰς πρὸς
52e ἡμᾶς αὐτοὺς καὶ ὁμολογίας παραβαίνεις, οὐχ ὑπὸ
ἀνάγκης ὁμολογήσας οὐδὲ ἀπατηθεὶς οὐδὲ ἐν ὀλίγῳ
χρόνῳ ἀναγκασθεὶς βουλεύσασθαι, ἀλλ' ἐν ἔτεσιν ἑβδομή-
κοντα, ἐν οἷς ἐξῆν σοι ἀπιέναι εἰ μὴ ἠρέσκομεν ἡμεῖς μηδὲ
e5 δίκαιαι ἐφαίνοντό σοι αἱ ὁμολογίαι εἶναι. σὺ δὲ οὔτε
Λακεδαίμονα προῃροῦ οὔτε Κρήτην, ἃς δὴ ἑκάστοτε φὴς
53a εὐνομεῖσθαι, οὔτε ἄλλην οὐδεμίαν τῶν Ἑλληνίδων πόλεων

11

ΠΛΑΤΩΝΟΣ

οὐδὲ τῶν βαρβάρων, ἀλλὰ ἐλάττω ἐξ αὐτῆς ἀπεδήμησας ἢ
οἱ χωλοί τε καὶ τυφλοὶ καὶ οἱ ἄλλοι ἀνάπηροι· οὕτω σοι
διαφερόντως τῶν ἄλλων Ἀθηναίων ἤρεσκεν ἡ πόλις τε καὶ
a5 ἡμεῖς οἱ νόμοι δῆλον ὅτι· τίνι γὰρ ἂν πόλις ἀρέσκοι ἄνευ
νόμων; νῦν δὲ δὴ οὐκ ἐμμενεῖς τοῖς ὡμολογημένοις; ἐὰν
ἡμῖν γε πείθῃ, ὦ Σώκρατες· καὶ οὐ καταγέλαστός γε ἔσῃ
ἐκ τῆς πόλεως ἐξελθών.
    "σκόπει γὰρ δή, ταῦτα παραβὰς καὶ ἐξαμαρτάνων τι
a10 τούτων τί ἀγαθὸν ἐργάσῃ σαυτὸν ἢ τοὺς ἐπιτηδείους τοὺς
53b σαυτοῦ. ὅτι μὲν γὰρ κινδυνεύσουσί γέ σου οἱ ἐπιτήδειοι καὶ
αὐτοὶ φεύγειν καὶ στερηθῆναι τῆς πόλεως ἢ τὴν οὐσίαν
ἀπολέσαι, σχεδόν τι δῆλον· αὐτὸς δὲ πρῶτον μὲν ἐὰν εἰς
τῶν ἐγγύτατά τινα πόλεων ἔλθῃς, ἢ Θήβαζε ἢ Μέγα-
b5 ράδε — εὐνομοῦνται γὰρ ἀμφότεραι — πολέμιος ἥξεις, ὦ
Σώκρατες, τῇ τούτων πολιτείᾳ, καὶ ὅσοιπερ κήδονται τῶν
αὑτῶν πόλεων ὑποβλέψονταί σε διαφθορέα ἡγούμενοι τῶν
νόμων, καὶ βεβαιώσεις τοῖς δικασταῖς τὴν δόξαν, ὥστε
53c δοκεῖν ὀρθῶς τὴν δίκην δικάσαι· ὅστις γὰρ νόμων δια-
φθορεύς ἐστιν σφόδρα που δόξειεν ἂν νέων γε καὶ ἀνοήτων
ἀνθρώπων διαφθορεὺς εἶναι. πότερον οὖν φεύξῃ τάς τε
εὐνομουμένας πόλεις καὶ τῶν ἀνδρῶν τοὺς κοσμιωτάτους;
c5 καὶ τοῦτο ποιοῦντι ἆρα ἄξιόν σοι ζῆν ἔσται; ἢ πλησιάσεις
τούτοις καὶ ἀναισχυντήσεις διαλεγόμενος — τίνας λόγους,
ὦ Σώκρατες; ἢ οὕσπερ ἐνθάδε, ὡς ἡ ἀρετὴ καὶ ἡ δικαιοσύνη πλείστου ἄξιον τοῖς ἀνθρώποις καὶ τὰ νόμιμα καὶ οἱ
νόμοι; καὶ οὐκ οἴει ἄσχημον φανεῖσθαι τὸ τοῦ Σωκράτους
53d πρᾶγμα; οἴεσθαί γε χρή. ἀλλ᾽ ἐκ μὲν τούτων τῶν τόπων
ἀπαρεῖς, ἥξεις δὲ εἰς Θετταλίαν παρὰ τοὺς ξένους τοὺς
Κρίτωνος; ἐκεῖ γὰρ δὴ πλείστη ἀταξία καὶ ἀκολασία, καὶ
ἴσως ἂν ἡδέως σου ἀκούοιεν ὡς γελοίως ἐκ τοῦ δεσμω-
d5 τηρίου ἀπεδίδρασκες σκευήν τέ τινα περιθέμενος ἢ
διφθέραν λαβὼν ἢ ἄλλα οἷα δὴ εἰώθασιν ἐνσκευάζεσθαι οἱ
ἀποδιδράσκοντες, καὶ τὸ σχῆμα τὸ σαυτοῦ μεταλλάξας·
ὅτι δὲ γέρων ἀνήρ, σμικροῦ χρόνου τῷ βίῳ λοιποῦ ὄντος
53e ὡς τὸ εἰκός, ἐτόλμησας οὕτω γλίσχρως ἐπιθυμεῖν ζῆν,
νόμους τοὺς μεγίστους παραβάς, οὐδεὶς ὃς ἐρεῖ; ἴσως, ἂν
μή τινα λυπῇς· εἰ δὲ μή, ἀκούσῃ, ὦ Σώκρατες, πολλὰ καὶ
ἀνάξια σαυτοῦ. ὑπερχόμενος δὴ βιώσῃ πάντας ἀνθρώπους
e5 καὶ δουλεύων — τί ποιῶν ἢ εὐωχούμενος ἐν Θετταλίᾳ,
ὥσπερ ἐπὶ δεῖπνον ἀποδεδημηκὼς εἰς Θετταλίαν; λόγοι δὲ
54a ἐκεῖνοι οἱ περὶ δικαιοσύνης τε καὶ τῆς ἄλλης ἀρετῆς ποῦ

12

ΚΡΙΤΩΝ

ἡμῖν ἔσονται; ἀλλὰ δὴ τῶν παίδων ἕνεκα βούλει ζῆν, ἵνα
αὐτοὺς ἐκθρέψῃς καὶ παιδεύσῃς; τί δέ; εἰς Θετταλίαν
αὐτοὺς ἀγαγὼν θρέψεις τε καὶ παιδεύσεις, ξένους ποιή-
a5   σας, ἵνα καὶ τοῦτο ἀπολαύσωσιν; ἢ τοῦτο μὲν οὔ, αὐτοῦ δὲ
τρεφόμενοι σοῦ ζῶντος βέλτιον θρέψονται καὶ παιδεύσονται μὴ συνόντος σοῦ αὐτοῖς; οἱ γὰρ ἐπιτήδειοι οἱ σοὶ
ἐπιμελήσονται αὐτῶν. πότερον ἐὰν εἰς Θετταλίαν
ἀποδημήσῃς, ἐπιμελήσονται, ἐὰν δὲ εἰς Ἅιδου
a10   ἀποδημήσῃς, οὐχὶ ἐπιμελήσονται; εἴπερ γέ τι ὄφελος
54b   αὐτῶν ἐστιν τῶν σοι φασκόντων ἐπιτηδείων εἶναι, οἴεσθαί
γε χρή.

"ἀλλ᾿, ὦ Σώκρατες, πειθόμενος ἡμῖν τοῖς σοῖς τροφεῦσι
μήτε παῖδας περὶ πλείονος ποιοῦ μήτε τὸ ζῆν μήτε ἄλλο
b5   μηδὲν πρὸ τοῦ δικαίου, ἵνα εἰς Ἅιδου ἐλθὼν ἔχῃς ταῦτα
πάντα ἀπολογήσασθαι τοῖς ἐκεῖ ἄρχουσιν· οὔτε γὰρ ἐνθάδε
σοι φαίνεται ταῦτα πράττοντι ἄμεινον εἶναι οὐδὲ δικαιότερον οὐδὲ ὁσιώτερον, οὐδὲ ἄλλῳ τῶν σῶν οὐδενί, οὔτε
ἐκεῖσε ἀφικομένῳ ἄμεινον ἔσται. ἀλλὰ νῦν μὲν ἠδικημένος
54c   ἄπει, ἐὰν ἀπίῃς, οὐχ ὑφ᾿ ἡμῶν τῶν νόμων, ἀλλὰ ὑπ᾿
ἀνθρώπων· ἐὰν δὲ ἐξέλθῃς οὕτως αἰσχρῶς ἀνταδικήσας τε
καὶ ἀντικακουργήσας, τὰς σαυτοῦ ὁμολογίας τε καὶ
συνθήκας τὰς πρὸς ἡμᾶς παραβὰς καὶ κακὰ ἐργασάμενος
c5   τούτους οὓς ἥκιστα ἔδει, σαυτόν τε καὶ φίλους καὶ πατρίδα
καὶ ἡμᾶς, ἡμεῖς τέ σοι χαλεπανοῦμεν ζῶντι, καὶ ἐκεῖ οἱ
ἡμέτεροι ἀδελφοὶ οἱ ἐν Ἅιδου νόμοι οὐκ εὐμενῶς σε
ὑποδέξονται, εἰδότες ὅτι καὶ ἡμᾶς ἐπεχείρησας ἀπολέσαι
54d   τὸ σὸν μέρος. ἀλλὰ μή σε πείσῃ Κρίτων ποιεῖν ἃ λέγει
μᾶλλον ἢ ἡμεῖς."

ταῦτα, ὦ φίλε ἑταῖρε Κρίτων, εὖ ἴσθι ὅτι ἐγὼ δοκῶ
ἀκούειν, ὥσπερ οἱ κορυβαντιῶντες τῶν αὐλῶν δοκοῦσιν
d5   ἀκούειν, καὶ ἐν ἐμοὶ αὕτη ἡ ἠχὴ τούτων τῶν λόγων βομβεῖ
καὶ ποιεῖ μὴ δύνασθαι τῶν ἄλλων ἀκούειν· ἀλλὰ ἴσθι, ὅσα
γε τὰ νῦν ἐμοὶ δοκοῦντα, ἐὰν λέγῃς παρὰ ταῦτα, μάτην
ἐρεῖς. ὅμως μέντοι εἴ τι οἴει πλέον ποιήσειν, λέγε.
ΚΡ. ἀλλ᾿, ὦ Σώκρατες, οὐκ ἔχω λέγειν.
54e   ΣΩ. ἔα τοίνυν, ὦ Κρίτων, καὶ πράττωμεν ταύτῃ,
ἐπειδὴ ταύτῃ ὁ θεὸς ὑφηγεῖται.

MORPHOLOGY AND SYNTAX

The following few pages, to which constant reference is made in the running commentary, focus on certain aspects of word-formation and syntactical structures. If you have an imperfect grasp of any of the areas covered, you will find it beneficial to study the data presented in the relevant section or sections *before* you embark on the text itself.

A. THE PERFECT AND PLUPERFECT

A.1
In Beginners' courses, the perfect and pluperfect generally crop up at a late stage, when there is mounting pressure to reach the final lesson. The former at any rate can prove a real distraction among other more general difficulties commonly encountered when an extended Greek text is tackled seriously for the first time. In fact, the perfect systems do not lend themselves to total assimilation within a very short time-span: one needs to work one's way into them, and to do that one has got to read a fair bit of Greek. A few moments spent (preferably with a set of paradigms illustrating the basic types by your side) on reviewing the perfects that actually occur in *Crito* may prove useful.

A.2
The important perfect εἰδέναι "to know" (from the same root as εἶδον, the aorist of ὁρᾶν) is so eccentric that it is better considered separately. We find:
Indicative 1st person singular οἶδα, 3rd person plural ἴσασιν
Infinitive already mentioned
Participle masculine plural εἰδότες
Imperative singular ἴσθι (3x)

A.3.a
— Active with *reduplication:*
Indicative 3rd singular κεκόμικεν (κομίζειν), λέληθεν (λανθάνειν); also active form γέγονεν, from γίγνεσθαι
Infinitive πεποιηκέναι (ποιεῖν)
Participle ἀπο-δεδημηκώς (ἀπο-δημεῖν)
— Active with *modified reduplication:*
Indicative 3rd singular πέφυκε (φύειν)
Infinitive δια-πεφευγέναι (δια-φεύγειν), τεθνάναι[1] (2x) ((ἀπο)θνῄσκειν)
— Active with *'Attic' reduplication* [2]:
Indicative 1st plural δι-εληλύθαμεν (δι-ιέναι/ δι-έρχομαι)

15

A.3.b

— Active with *(modified) augmentation/ irregularities:*

Indicative 1st singular ἑώρακα[3] (ὁρᾶν), 2nd singular εἴωθας[4] (ἔθειν), 3rd singular εἴωθεν, ἔοικεν (infinitive ἐοικέναι), 3rd plural εἰώθασιν

Infinitive ὡμολογηκέναι (2x) (ὁμολογεῖν)

Participle masculine ὡμολογηκώς, feminine παρ-εστώσῃ[5], neuter εἰκός (2x) (ἐοικέναι see above)

A.4

— Middle, only:

Indicative 2nd singular ἀφ-ῖξαι* (2x) & 3rd singular ἀφ-ῖκται* (2x) (ἀφικνεῖσθαι)

Infinitive βεβουλεῦσθαι (βουλεύεσθαι)

A.5

— Passive:

Indicative 3rd singular δέδοκται* (2x) (δοκεῖν), εὐεργέτηται (εὐεργετεῖν), also 3rd plural formed with participle ἐκ-κεχυμέναι εἰσίν (ἐκ-χεῖν)

Infinitive ἀνα-τετράφθαι* (ἀνα-τρέπειν), πεπρᾶχθαι* (3x) (πράττειν), ἐστερῆσθαι[6] (στερεῖν)

Participle ἠδικημένος (ἀδικεῖν), ὡμολογημένοις (ὁμολογεῖν), δι-εφθαρμένου[6] (3x) (δια-φθείρειν), τεταγμένοι* (τάττειν) — Also 'periphrastic' subjunctive, formed with participle: 3rd singular δια-βεβλημένος (δια-βάλλειν) ᾖ

A.6

The past of the perfect, the pluperfect, occurs once only: 3rd singular ὡμολόγητο

---

[1] A 'second perfect' form ('first': τεθνηκέναι). See also note on 43c9-d1. [2] Where a verb beginning with a vowel reduplicates the initial vowel *and* consonant and lengthens the vowel that follows reduplication: as ἀκούω perf. ἀκήκοα. [3] Note the twin augmentation (with the aspirate retained), found also in imperfect ἑώρων. [4] Cf. the related ἐθίζειν, with perfects εἴθικα & εἴθισμαι. [5] A 'second perfect'; see note on 43b8-9. The 'first perfect' form, ἑστηκώς -υῖα -ός, is not at all common in Classical Greek. [6] Note the presence of ἑ-, -ε- here: due to the particular consonant-combinations heading the respective stems.

* The indicative paradigm for πεπρᾶχθαι runs: πέπραγμαι, πέπραξαι, πέπρακται, πεπράγμεθα, πέπραχθε, πεπραγμένοι εἰσί. Identical or related euphonic changes apply to the endings of τεταγμένοι, and to those of δέδοκται, ἀφῖξαι and ἀφῖκται. Differently -τετράφθαι (stem ends in labial plosive π; before σθ, σ is suppressed and labial becomes φ).

B. VERBAL ADJECTIVES

B.1

It is important to grasp the function of verbal adjectives in -τέος: they play an important part in Plato's writings. The 19 examples in *Crito* are all the neuter singular nominative, and in nearly every case one must supply the verbal element "it is/ is it?" (cf. the note on 43d7-8); exceptions: 48c8 subjunctive ᾖ, 49a4 (-5) infinitive εἶναι in indirect speech.

B.2

To construct one, add -τέον to the stem of the aorist passive (or middle-passive) infinitive, changing terminal θ, φ and χ to τ, π and κ where appropriate. Thus ἀδικεῖν *(do wrong)* will produce ἀδικητέον (aorist passive infinitive ἀδικη-θῆναι), πράττειν *(carry out)* πρακτέον (aorist passive infinitive πραχ-θῆναι).

B.3

You will encounter the following:

1. ἀδικητέον 2x (see above)
2. ἀναχωρητέον (ἀνα-χωρεῖν *retreat*; ~ -χωρηθῆναι)
3. γυμναστέον (γυμνάζεσθαι *train*; ~ γυμνασθῆναι)
4. ἐδεστέον (ἔδειν *eat*; ~ ἐδεσθῆναι)
5. ἐξαπατητέον (ἐξ-απατᾶν *practise deception*; ~ ἐξαπατηθῆναι)
6. λειπτέον (λείπειν *leave*; ~ λειφθῆναι)
7. ποιητέον 5x (ποιεῖν *do*; ~ ποιηθῆναι)
8. ποτέον (πίνειν *drink*; ~ ποθῆναι)
9. πρακτέον 2x (see above)
10. σκεπτέον 2x (σκοπεῖν/ σκέπτεσθαι *consider*; ~ σκεφθῆναι)
11. ὑπεικτέον (ὑπ-είκειν *give way, yield*; ~ ὑπ-ειχθῆναι)
12. φροντιστέον (φροντίζειν *consider, take into account*; ~ φροντισθῆναι)

B.4

One may think of ἀδικητέον in terms of δεῖ ἀδικεῖν (grammarians are fond of adducing 51b10-c1, where ποιητέον is followed up with πείθειν, viz. <δεῖ> πείθειν), "it is necessary/one must/ ought to do wrong". In line with this it is possible to employ a verbal adjective with an accusative of the personal agent, "by": see 49a4. However, more commonly, the dative is used: 47b9, 48a5, c7-8.

B.5

Formations derived from transitive verbs may, naturally enough, govern an accusative: so 46b3-4 ταῦτα πρακτέον, and a further 8 times.

C. ARTICULAR INFINITIVE

C.1

The neuter singular of the definite article is a natural ally of the infinitive, which functions as a verbal noun. So τὸ νικᾶν, "the act of winning", "the attainment of victory", "the capacity/ tendency to win" etc., in negative form τὸ μὴ νικᾶν, "non-attainment of victory", "failure/ inability to win" etc.

C.2

Tenses. Of the 17 examples in *Crito,* 14 are present active, 1 is present middle, 1 is perfect active, 1 is perfect passive. Thus τὸ ἀδικεῖν, "the act of doing wrong", "wrongdoing", τὸ ἐρωτᾶν καὶ ἀποκρίνεσθαι, "the practice/ technique of question and answer". But τὸ πεποιηκέναι, "the act/ step of having made", τὸ ἐστερῆσθαι, "the fact of having been (being) deprived".

C.3

Flexibility. The articular infinitive is used in the nominative as subject of the sentence (49a5-6, b4, c7), in the genitive as subject of a genitive absolute (49d8), in the accusative as object of a transitive verb (48b5, 54b4), in the genitive in conjunction with διαφέρειν *differ from* (49c7), in the dative in conjunction with χρῆσθαι *use* (50c10), as an independent dative of means (51d2), in cases governed by various prepositions (accusative 43a7-8, genitive 44b8, 46e3, 48d5-6).

C.4

Linked with adverbs: 43a7-8, 48b5 (cf. id. 7), 49c7.

C.5

The infinitival element in its turn can govern accusative (49c7, 51d2), genitive (44b8-9), infinitive (46e3-47a1).

C.6

43c3, with double negative μὴ οὐ, requires separate consideration: see the note on c2-3.

D. SYNTAX OF THE SUBJUNCTIVE

D.1

Subjunctives are so widespread in Plato that it is essential to have a firm grasp of their behaviour. There follows a review of the various ways in which they are deployed in *Crito.* Two are of overriding importance.

D.2

The first of these involves the use of ἐάν i.e. εἰ + ἄν (20x), alternative form ἄν [ᾱ] (4x), crasis κἄν (1x), with negative μή, in two chief ways:

(i) To express a prospective condition of the kind "[*protasis*] If you do so [viz. at some point in the future], [*apodosis*] you will be punished". Example: 53b3-5 ἐὰν ... ἔλθῃς, ... ἥξεις ... The apodosis carries a future tense also in 51a5-6, 54a9, 10, c1, 6/8, d8, but a variety of other leading verbs are possible too (e.g. present indicative 44b8, imperative 46c3, hortatory subjunctive 48c2); with verb suppressed: 50c5, 53a6, 53e2.

(ii) Less commonly (though in practice one usage is sometimes hard to differentiate from the other), to express a general condition or supposition. Example: 44d4-5 "They are capable of ... ἐάν τις ... διαβεβλημένος ᾖ", "if a person has been ...". Cf. its use at 47d8ff., in support of a proposition.

— Further points to note:

(i) οὐδ' ἄν + subjunctive is used to signify not "not even if *x* were to happen" but rather "not even if *x* happens": 46c3-5, 49c11.

(ii) At 48e5-49a1 ἐάν means "to see whether (*x* proves to be)".

(iii) Duplicated ἐάντε can function like εἴτε ... εἴτε, "whether ... or": see the notes on 51b5-6 and 51d7-8.

D.3

The other way in which the subjunctive is worked particularly hard is in the formation of indefinite clauses in primary sequence, type "Whoever does this is automatically put to death" (remember that English often dispenses with the indefinite suffix "-ever"). Seven such clauses are packed into the stretch from 51d3 to 52a2.

The subjunctive (negative μή) is found in combination with the particle ἄν and the following introductory words:

(i) Relative pronoun ὅς ἥ ὅ etc. (12x, and relative adverb ᾗ "as" 2x); (neuter of ὅστις, "whoever") ὅτι (2x), ἄττ(α) = neuter plural ἅτινα (1x)

(ii) ὅποι "whither" (3x)

(iii) ὥσπερ "just as", "in the way in which" (1x; see note on 44c8-9)

(iv) ἐπειδάν = ἐπειδή + ἄν, "whenever" (1x)

D.4

Purpose clauses: "in order to" etc. Five cases, all introduced by ἵνα (no ἄν! Negative μή 1x), four of them in primary sequence, one (43b6) in historic (the so-called "vivid" use of the subjunctive, uncommon in Plato; here specifying a condition *continuing into the present*).

D.5

The following are all akin to the use of (ὅπως) μή + subjunctive to express the notion of prospective fear or apprehension: (i) 44e2-4 προμηθῇ ... μὴ παρέχωσιν ... "feel concern ..., in the fear that they may cause ..."; 45e1-2 αἰσχύνομαι μὴ δόξῃ ... "feel shame, anxious as I am that it may be thought ...". (ii) 46a3-4 ὅρα μὴ ... ᾖ "watch that it is not", and so 49c11-d2 ὅρα ... ὅπως μὴ ... ὁμολογῇς "watch that you don't agree".

D.6

The so-called "independent uses" of the subjunctive are well represented, thus:

(i) Exhortation, 1st person plural, "let us": 48c2 πειρώμεθα ... ἐῶμεν, "let's make the attempt (otherwise) let's drop it"; more at 48d9, 54e1.

(ii) Prohibition, aorist, either 2nd person singular (45b6-7 μήτε ... ἀποκάμῃς), or 3rd (54d1 μή σε πείσῃ Κρίτων ποιεῖν, "don't let Crito talk you into doing").

(iii) (a) Tentative statement involving μή (negative μὴ οὐ) + 3rd person singular subjunctive, "perhaps ..." etc. (3x: see note on 48c4-5). (b) Emphatic denial, οὐ μή + 1st person aorist subjunctive, "I most certainly won't ..." (1x: see note on 46c3).

19

iv) Deliberative use (type "What are we to do?"): 52d6/7, in an indirect question 48d7-8, 49d6.

D.7

The forms employed require only selective comment:

(i) Verbs in -ναι: 3rd singular ᾖ (εἶναι) (3x); 2nd singular ἀπίῃς and 1st plural δι-ῑῶμεν from -ιέναι (viz. oblique forms of indicative -έρχομαι, cf. note on 53e4); 1st plural φῶμεν (φάναι).

(ii) Among verbs in -ειν, we find aorist passives 3rd singular δοκιμασθῇ (δοκιμάζειν) & πραχθῇ (πράττειν), 1st plural ἀναγκασθῶμεν (ἀναγκάζειν); perfect passive subjunctive δια-βεβλημένος ᾖ (δια-βάλλειν), see above A.5 ad fin.

E. SYNTAX OF THE OPTATIVE

E.1

Optatives in *Crito* are fewer in number (34: subjunctives 75) and simpler to deal with.

E.2

(i) ἄν + optative in hypothetical statements or questions ("potential" optative). Type: "It would (could should etc.) be/ would it be ... (?)", occasionally "It must be ...", "It is surely ..."; negative οὐ. 22 examples in all.

(ii) This brand of optative + ἄν in the *apodosis,* εἰ + optative in the *protasis* in a condition of the type "If I were to do this, you would be angry". So 50c7-8, 52a6-7. — In 46b1-2 such a protasis is preceded by a blunt statement of fact (see note); in 46c7-8 & 50a6-8 the εἰ clause can be translated by "suppose we/ they were to ..."; in 51d7 similarly εἰ μή can be represented by "supposing that ... not".

E.3

45b8: a deliberative subjunctive (above, D.6 (iv)) turned into an optative due to "assimilation", see the note there. — 50e9: indefinite (cf. above, D.3), after *past* leading verb. — 46d9-e1 optative generated by indirect speech with leading verb in the past; a related usage at 52c7.

E.4

Points to note on forms:

(i) It is advisable to be familiar with the optative of φάναι: in *Crito:* 1st singular φαίην (2x), 3rd singular φαίη (2x), 3rd plural φαῖεν (3x).

(ii) See the notes on ἐνέγκαιμι at 43c7-8, χρῷο at 45b8-c1.

NOTES

Before looking at each portion of the text, study the Vocabulary provided for it. It lists a number of words which are well worth committing to memory; those of lesser importance are dealt with in the running commentary. *Not* included are the very commonest words: any still unfamiliar to you as you work through the text should be looked up (try Liddell and Scott's *Intermediate Greek Lexicon*), jotted down and memorised at the earliest opportunity.

"*MS*" refers to the introductory notes on Morphology and Syntax.

Synopsis

Socrates, in prison awaiting execution, is visited by his friend Crito. After some discussion about its likely date, Crito urges Socrates to consent to being got out of prison: otherwise, what would people think? Socrates has hard words to say on the subject of public opinion: after rejecting further appeals he reverts to the question of what, and whose, opinions matter, concluding that only the opinion of the expert in any given field — morality included, since here such fearful damage can be inflicted that life would not be worth living — is worthy of regard. The question to be addressed is: is it *right* or *not right* to escape? Crito has to admit that one's conduct has to be guided by what is right. Imagine what would happen, Socrates adds, if the Laws of the city were to confront him. Their case would be unanswerable: "You cannot destroy us and your city but are obliged by virtue of the fact that your continued residence is tantamount to approval of the legal system obtaining here to obey us, or to *persuade* us of the rightness of any action you envisage which contravenes what is laid down by law. Besides, by running away you will endanger your friends, harm your children and be regarded with suspicion in any law-abiding city". Crito has no counter-arguments to offer. Socrates then must follow the course directed by "god".

43a

399 BC. Socrates, in prison awaiting the carrying out of the death sentence imposed by the court a few weeks earlier, wakes an hour or two before dawn to find that he has a visitor, his old friend Crito.

Vocabulary
Nouns

δεσμωτήριον, τό	prison
φύλαξ-ακος, ὁ	guard, warder

21

Verbs

ὑπ-ακούειν — respond (to one [dative]), answer the door (to someone)

φοιτᾶν — visit regularly, frequent

εὐ-εργετεῖν — confer a benefit, do a good turn

Adverbs

ἐπιεικῶς — [+ adjective or adverb] quite, pretty, fairly

ἄρτι — just now, lately

πρῴ — early

Aids to comprehension

43a1

τηνικάδε: "at this (particular) time/ hour"; there follows shortly a related interrogative, πηνίκα, "at what hour?".

ἀφῖξαι: A second person singular perfect, from ἀφικνεῖσθαι, see *MS* A.4.

ἦ [rather than ἤ]: An affirmative or emphasising particle ("indeed", "surely", "why"), here as often linked with οὐ (cf. 50d7) in prefacing a question to which a positive answer is confidently expected. Without negative: 43c9, 50c5, 53c7.

πρῴ: Socrates' daily visitors normally had to wait around, because the prison was opened up οὐ πρῴ (*Phaedo* 59c5-6).

a2 πάνυ μὲν οὖν: This and very similar expressions are employed in Platonic dialogue to indicate total assent: "absolutely". (Founded on the use of the combination μὲν οὖν to *correct* or *contradict* a previous utterance; some take Crito to be saying here: "on the contrary, very <early>" or if you like, "very <early>, actually".)

a3 μάλιστα: Here "roughly", "approximately" (so often with numerals).

a4 ὄρθρος βαθύς: Not, as it is often translated, "just before daybreak". ὄρθρος denotes the period of darkness (2-3 hours) running up to dawn, when it is still too dark to see; βαθύς, "deep", reinforces the point that it is indeed early: there is still some way to go before sunrise.

a5 ὅπως: "how it came about that": πῶς may often be translated by our "how come?", see 43b1.

ἠθέλησε: Note the aorist (cf. on 44c4-5): "proved, showed himself willing".

a7-8 συνήθης: Adjective of ἀληθής type: "used" to or "well acquainted" with.

διὰ τὸ ... φοιτᾶν: Articular infinitive (see *MS* C.3-4): "due to my ...-ing". For the fact see *Phaedo* 59d1ff. (where this same verb φοιτᾶν is used).

καί τι καὶ ...: καί ... καί means "and into the bargain". εὐεργετεῖν τι, "confer some/ a<n unspecified> benefit" is here presented in passive form; postpositive τι occupies the expected second place. εὐεργέτηται (subject the warder) is a third person singular perfect passive, see *MS* A.5.

22

43b

Crito has deliberately not disturbed Socrates' sleep; he can only marvel at his friend's imperturbability at this hour.

Vocabulary

Nouns

ἀγρυπνία, ἡ	state of wakefulness
συμφορά, ἡ	calamity
λύπη, ἡ	grief, depression
σιγή, ἡ	silence; dative -ῇ silently

Verbs

δι-άγειν	pass the time
ἐγείρειν & ἐπ-εγείρειν	wake (somebody) up
εὐδαιμονίζειν	consider/ pronounce fortunate
καθ-εύδειν	sleep
τελευτᾶν	finish, end <one's life: see 43d6>
ἀγανακτεῖν	feel indignation [+ dat., "at"], take it hard
παρα-καθ-ῆσθαι	sit by (someone's) side

Adverbs

πρᾴως	mildly, placidly
εἶτα	[temporal] then ; [in argument] well then
ἐπίτηδες	deliberately, on purpose

Asseverative particle

μά	ναί μά literally = "yes by", οὐ μά "no by": both with accusative case.

Aids to comprehension

43b1-2

πῶς: See on 43a5.

ἀλλά: This particle, "but <rather>", can often be translated "instead of ..."

παρακάθησαι: The present tense of this verb runs -ημαι -ησαι -ηται etc.; "sit" in Greek frequently carries the implication "sit doing nothing, idly".

b3 οὐ μὰ τὸν Δία: In modern terms, e.g., "Heavens above, no! <Of course I didn't wake you up!>"

b3-4 οὐδ᾽ ἂν αὐτός ... :"nor would I myself want to be (be out of choice) ....". Imperfect + ἄν (cf. 44d8, 52b3-4): "would be doing" ~ aorist + ἄν: "would have done".

b4-5 ἀλλὰ ... θαυμάζω: καί not just with σοῦ, but with the whole of this clause: "but [he changes the subject, and speaks of Socrates' sleep in positive terms] I in fact have for some while been surprised at you ..." (Socrates had expressed *his surprise* at Crito's admission, θαυμάζω ... 43a5). The genitive with this verb denotes the cause: "at". πάλαι + *present* is the usual way of saying "I *have* long been ..."

ὡς: The behaviour of this word takes some getting used to. Here "how" (for related uses see 44b4, 45e3/4), at 43b9 "<seeing> how"; but at 43b6 with superlative adverb, "as ... as possible", "in the -est way imaginable".

b6 οὐκ ἤγειρον: Imperfect this time (ctr. b1; ἐπ-: the preverb is often dropped when a verb is repeated after a short interval): "I was not for waking", "didn't feel inclined to wake".

ἵνα ... διάγῃς: Purpose clause, with subjunctive after leading verb in *past* tense: see *MS* D.4.

b6-8 καὶ .. μὲν δή .. καὶ ...: The first καί is connective, the second = "as well <as on the present occasion>" (since that will be specified shortly, this καί can be bypassed in translation). μέν looks forward to δέ in line 8; δή lends emphasis to πολλάκις.

τοῦ τρόπου: Another example (cf.43b4) of a genitive expressing ground or cause: "in your ..."

b8-9 πολὺ ... μάλιστα: πολύ is adverbial, lit. "much the most"; this might be rendered "<I consider you so> more than ever ..."

τῇ νῦν ...: The familiar use of article + adverb + participle, best translated with a relative clause in English, "which at the present time ..."

παρ-εστώσῃ: παρεστώς -ῶσα -ός is the perfect participle (cf. *MS* A.3.b) of παριστάναι, used intransitively to denote something untoward that "has confronted" or "confronts" one: cf. παρούσῃ at 43c3.

b10-11 καὶ γὰρ ἄν ... εἴη: καὶ γάρ expresses strong assent: : "<Yes,> because it would in fact *or* indeed be ..."

πλημμελές: Literally "out of tune", here something like "wholly inappropriate/ improper"; followed up with accusative + infinitive, "that <a person> of such an age should ..."

τηλικοῦτον: Socrates was 70 (52e3-4, cf. *Apology* 17d2); in id. 33d10 S. speaks of C. as ἐμὸς ἡλικιώτης [cf. below, c2-3] καὶ δημότης, i.e. the same age as himself and a member of the same deme.

εἰ: Cf. the note on 52c6-7.

43c-d

There is a very good reason for Crito's early appearance: once the ship from Delos arrives [see Phaedo 58a10-c5 for an extended account], as it will imminently, the execution can go ahead.

Vocabulary

Nouns

ἡλικία, ἡ	age, years
ἐπιτήδειος, ὁ	close friend
πλοῖον, τό	sailing vessel, boat

Verb

ἀλίσκεσθαι	be caught (ἐν, in, up in)

Adverbs

αὔριον	tomorrow; εἰς αὔριον come tomorrow
τήμερον	today
ταύτῃ	in this fashion

Aids to comprehension

43c2-3

οὐδὲν αὐτοὺς ἐπιλύεται ... τὸ μὴ οὐχὶ ἀγανακτεῖν: "in no way affords them release/relief from a sense of indignation". An articular infinitive (cf. *MS* C) with *double* negative μὴ οὐ can follow *negatived* verbs denoting "hinder", "restrain", "refrain" etc.: οὐκ εἴργει σε τὸ μὴ οὐ τοῦτο ποιεῖν, "he does not prevent you from doing this".

τῇ παρούσῃ τύχῃ: See on 43b8-9.

c4 ἔστι ταῦτα: Neuter plural subject, singular verb. ἔστι (with this accent) = "is the case", "is true".

δή strengthens the interrogative: "*why* is it that ..." Socrates now harks back to his very first question.

ἀφῖξαι: *MS* A.4.

c7-8 ἐν τοῖς: An idiomatic expression (again at 52a5, 7), simply serving to strengthen the superlative adverb: "most ... of all", "more ... than anyone".

ἐνέγκαιμι: First person singular aorist optative of φέρειν.

c9 τίνα ταύτην; Supply from above φέρων ἀφῖξαι.

c9-d1 ἦ: Cf. on 43a1. "Is it indeed the case that ...?"

ἀφῖκται: *MS* A.4.

οὗ .. ἀφικομένου: Genitive absolute, "which <vessel> having arrived", i.e. "on the arrival of which"; the principal verb δεῖ, expressing the all-important notion of inevitability, is allowed to cut into this unit.

τεθνάναι: Perfect infinitive (see *MS* A.3.a) of (ἀπο)θνῄσκειν; "to die", the perfect here stressing the finality of the process.

43d2

οὔ(-)τοι δή ...: "It has not actually [δή] arrived, I can assure you of that [τοι]".

δοκεῖν μέν μοι: Absolute infinitive, as in the common ὡς εἰπεῖν: "to my way of thinking". μέν here has no answering δέ, as is often the case when it is

25

associated with words expressing opinion, "implicitly contrasted with certainty or reality" as J.D. Denniston puts it (*The Greek Particles* 382).

ἥξει: ἥξειν all manuscripts. Some have infinitive δοκεῖν as well; δοκεῖ others, an attempt to restore coherence.

d3 ἐξ ὧν ἀπαγγέλλουσιν: A clear instance of "relative attraction" (cf. 50a2-3, 50c6-7, 51c9-d1), compressing ἐκ τούτων ἅ ...: "judging by what they report".

Σουνίου: Cape Sunium: the SE tip of Attica. The vessel had taken shelter there, the winds being unfavourable at the time (*Phaedo* 58b8ff.).

d4-5 ἐκ τούτων τῶν ἀγγέλων: If ἐκ τούτων alone had been transmitted, the text would never have been questioned: "from this", corresponding to ἐξ ὧν ... in d3; and many editors excise τῶν ἀγγέλων, regarding it (cf. the minority variant τῶν ἀγγελιῶν, "messages") as an explanatory note which has found its way into the text. But a deliberate-sounding "it's clear then from what these messengers say" is quite in keeping with Crito's anxious state of mind.

d5-6 ἀνάγκη ... is followed up with accusative and infinitive (cf. the use of δεῖ), i.e. it will be inevitable/ inevitably follow beyond any doubt (δή) that ...

d7-8 ἀλλ᾽ indicates acquiescence, "well".

τύχῃ ἀγαθῇ: Literally "<may it be> to the accompaniment of good fortune". This is a way of saying (if there is meant to be a pause after ἀγαθῇ) "let's hope that it all turns out for the best". With a comma after ἀγαθῇ (as in the printed text): "if the gods want it this way, then (and the outcome will be a happy one, one hopes) so be it".

φίλον: Supply "is". The third person singular of the verb "to be", "is", "it is", "there is" and so on, is commonly suppressed, particularly in brief utterances (so too, though less often, the plural, cf. on 44d8, 45a8-9, 45b3; first person singular 46b4). This habit will be noted only sporadically henceforth.

ἔστω: Third person singular imperative of εἶναι, "let it be", cf. ἐχέτω 44e1; γενέσθω 45b8.

44a-c5

Socrates has had a dream indicating that the ship will arrive somewhat later than Crito supposes. But, the latter insists, Socrates must consent to being got out of prison — he does not want people to think that he has put money before friends.

Vocabulary
Nouns

καιρός, ὁ	right time, opportune moment
ἐνύπνιον, τό	dream-vision, dream
ἱμάτια, τά	clothes

Adjectives

ἄτοπος	out of the way, strange, odd
κύριος	exercising control *or* authority over [genitive]
ἐναργής	(crystal-) clear
εὐειδής	physically attractive

Verbs

ἀν-αλίσκειν	spend
κινδυνεύειν	+ infinitive (be in danger of [so at 53b1], but also) used to express likelihood or probability
τεκμαίρεσθαι	arrive at a judgement on, infer
ἀμελεῖν	be negligent, neglect
προθυμεῖσθαι	desire earnestly, be enthusiastically committed to a course of action
στερεῖσθαι	be deprived (of, genitive)
ἔοικε(ν)	[cf. *MS* A.3.b] it seems
ἐπ-ιέναι	[~ ἐπέρχομαι] (of time) approach, draw near
οἷός (οἵα οἷόν) τ᾿ εἶναι	be able, capable

Adverbs

ἐνθένδε	from this place, hence
λίαν	too much, too

Preposition

χωρίς	(+ genitive) apart from

Particles

καίτοι	and yet
τοίνυν	(well) then, so [cf. also note on 52c4]

Aids to comprehension

44a1

πόθεν: "from what place?", hence "on what basis?", "on what grounds?"

a2 ἐρῶ: First person singular future of λέγω.

a2-3 γάρ: Commonly used after expressions like "I'll tell you (the truth)", "pay attention". English can generally do without any transitional word.

που: "I believe", "if I am not mistaken".

... ὑστεραίᾳ [supply ἡμέρᾳ] ... ἧ ᾖ ἂν ...: Dative of time; literally "on the <day coming> later than [next after] <that> on which [whenever it is: indefinite clause: *MS* D.3] ..."

a4 φασί: φάναι frequently = "say so", "say yes" (cf. on 49b5).

γέ τοι δή: γε commonly marks assent (cf. on 44b6), and in combination with τοι can bear the sense "at any rate". So here: "Yes, that's certainly [δή] what ... say anyway".

οἱ τούτων κύριοι: A vague way of referring to "The Eleven", officials in charge of the Athenian police and prisons, with responsibility for executions.

a5-6 τῆς ἐπιούσης ἡμέρας ...: Genitive of time, = in the course of, during a specified period.

τῆς ἑτέρας (ἡμέρας): ἕτερος = "the other one", in this case the next in line, the day after the one about to begin.

a6 ἐνυπνίου: Socrates on dreams: see *Apology* 33c5ff., *Phaedo* 60e1ff.

a7 ἑώρακα: First person singular perfect (*MS* A.3.b) of ὁρᾶν.

a7-8 κινδυνεύεις ... με: i.e. your *not* waking me, it seems, was most opportune. τινι here gives emphasis, as in (e.g.) σὺν τάχει τινι, "with a <considerable> degree of speed".

a9 ἦν ...: The word-order (note postponed interrogative) should be reflected in translation: "and just what was it, this dream?". δή highlights the speaker's keen interest.

44b1

καλέσαι: Aorist infinitive active of καλεῖν: note the irregular ε.

b3 An adaptation of Homer, *Iliad* 9.363, the Thessalian Achilles speaking of getting home (Socrates himself will soon be heading for "home") from Troy, with first person verb ἱκοίμην, "Come the third day I would/ should reach rich-clodded Phthia". [*Homerica:* ἦμαρ-ατος, τό, day; κεν for ἄν; τρίτατος = τρίτος; ἐρίβωλος having an abundance (ἐρι- like περι-, to express richness, plenty) of clods (βῶλοι); ἵκοιο for ἀφίκοιο, here (as commonly in poetry) used with a simple accusative marking destination.]

b4 ὡς: Exclamatory, "how ...!"

ἄτοπον ...: Supply "is".

b5 μὲν οὖν: "rather", "on the contrary" (see on 43a2).

ὥς γε: "as at any rate": "or so it seems to me".

b6 γε expresses agreement (cf. 44a4, 48a4) and gives extra emphasis: "yes, all too ..."

b6-7 ἀλλ᾽ followed by an imperative (very common): "(but) come", "come on now".

δαιμόνιε: You can be called δαιμόνιος if you do something so abnormal or incomprehensible that the supernatural must be presumed to be at work; often used in (affectionate) rebuke. Cf. on μακάριε at 44c6, θαυμάσιε at 48b2.

ἔτι καὶ νῦν: Literally "still even now", i.e. even at this late hour.

ἐμοὶ πιθοῦ not πιθοῦ μοι: do what *I* tell you <instead of following your own inclinations>.

σώθητι is imperative singular of the aorist passive of σῴζειν.

b7 ὡς: "because", as at 45d9, 46b4, 48e3 (second ὡς).

ἐὰν .. ἀποθάνῃς: Prospective conditional, see *MS* D.2.

b8-9 τοῦ ἐστερῆσθαι: Articular infinitive (*MS* C.2, 3, 5; verbal form: id. A.5), lit. "the act/ fact of being deprived".

τοῦ: The MSS have σοῦ: τοῦ neatly restores sense. <τοῦ> σοῦ has been suggested, but a pronoun is not needed.

οἷον: It is essential to grasp the function of this word: it is a *qualitative relative*, picking up τοιούτου, "the sort of person who", "the like of whom"; cf. 45d3, 53d6.

οὐδένα μή ποτε εὑρήσω: οὐ (here absorbed by οὐδένα) μή + future indicative (far more often, aorist subjunctive, cf. 46c3) is used to make a strong negative declaration: "certainly not, not for sure".

b9-10 ἔτι δέ: ἔτι often means "further", "more than that". A more logical antecedent to "and on top of that I shall be thought" would have been "in the first place I shall be deprived of you ...".

οἳ ... ἴσασιν: οἵ is best taken as a *causal* relative, μή because the subject is a generality (πολλοί): "as being people who don't know".

ἐμὲ καὶ σέ: The normal Greek order of priority: "me" comes first.

ἴσασιν: Cf. *MS* A.2.

b10-c2 ὡς here closely with the participle, "I shall be thought, as one who was <in their perception> capable of ..., to have neglected you"; since he clearly had the money (Crito was a wealthy man: cf. *Euthydemus* 304c3f., and *Phaedo* 115d6ff.), it must have been negligence, so they'll conclude.

44c2

αἰσχίων ... δοκεῖν: αἰσχίων is the irregular comparative of αἰσχρός: "a more ... reputation than this [the common "genitive of comparison"], <I mean> than [ἤ] to have the reputation of ..."

c3 περὶ πλείονος [irregular comparative of πολύς] ποιεῖσθαι [middle]: A common idiomatic expression (cf. 54b4), "to estimate at a greater price", "value more highly"; περὶ πολλοῦ (45c3, 46e1, 48e4) and πλείστου (cf. 48b5) also occur frequently.

c4-5 πείσονται ... ὡς: Future of πείθομαι, "be convinced, believe that"; see on 47c3.

οὐκ ἠθέλησας: Aorist, "you refused" (outright).

ἡμῶν προθυμουμένων: Genitive absolute, bringing the plea to a forceful close: "although we ..."

44c6-d

Socrates firmly rejects the proposition that the "opinion of the many" is worth bothering about.

Vocabulary
Adjectives

φρόνιμος	prudent, intelligent; *opposite* ἄφρων-ονος
ἐπιεικής	reasonable, fair-minded, enlightened

Verbs

δια-βάλλειν	misrepresent
μέλειν	See below
φροντίζειν	(+ genitive) give consideration to, regard
(ἐξ)εργάζεσθαι	perform, carry out
ἡγεῖσθαι	suppose, hold

Adverb

σχεδόν	almost, just about

Aids to comprehension
44c6-7

ἡμῖν ... δόξης μέλει: The verb is employed impersonally, μέλει μοι τούτου, "there is a concern to me of (about) this", i.e. "I am concerned about this". The use of μέλειν in d2 below still comes under this heading, despite the absence of a dative: "that there should be concern about".

μακάριε: Cf. on δαιμόνιε at 44b6. Socrates responds with an ὦ μακάριε, lit. "blessed one"; this mode of address too harbours a tone of (polite) remonstrance: "my *dear* Crito".

c8-9 αὐτά commonly means "the topic in hand", "the thing (matter, point) under consideration"; we might say here "this whole business".

οὕτω ... πραχθῇ: πεπρᾶχθαι is a perfect infinitive passive (cf. *MS* A.5), πραχθῇ a third person singular (after neuter plural subject) aorist passive subjunctive. "... to have been managed exactly as it has been managed <whatever precise form that might take: hence indefinite ἄν + subjunctive: *MS* D.3>".

44d1

δή: "you see of course", "you *do* see".

d2-3 αὐτὰ ... ὅτι: Prepositive αὐτός = "-self" (etc.): "the very <troubles> which are present (confront us) right now <are> clear (indicate clearly) that ..."

d4-5 ἐάν with subjunctive to express a general supposition (cf. *MS* D.2), "if an individual has been misrepresented <in a court of law> among them" — as Socrates himself has been. Cf. *Apology* 18d2-3.

διαβεβλημένος: Perfect passive participle, combined with ᾖ to form subjunctive (*MS* A.5; D.7).

d6 εἰ γὰρ ὤφελον: ὤφελον *ought* is aorist of ὀφείλειν, used in this formula (or with εἴθε in place of εἰ γάρ) to express (in this case) a present unattained wish: "one wishes that they were capable ..."

d7 ἵνα οἷοί τ' ἦσαν: ἵνα with indicative: the imperfect (aorist or pluperfect if the reference is to past time) is deployed in cases where the action of the main verb is not fulfilled, so that the purpose is not achievable: "so that they were capable also ..."

d8 καὶ καλῶς ἂν εἶχεν: "and then it (all) would be well (fine)". ἔχειν with adverb = "be". Imperfect + ἄν: cf. on 43b3-4.

νῦν δέ: As often, "but as things stand", "but as it is".

οὐδέτερα means "neither of two things, courses" etc.

οἷοί τε: Supply "are", cf. next line; and an infinitive from above.

d9-10 ... ὅτι ἂν τύχωσι: "they do this, <viz.> whatever they chance [indefinite clause, *MS* D.3] <to do>", i.e. "they act in an entirely random fashion".

44e-45a5

Is Socrates concerned about the punitive measures that might be taken against Crito and others if they secured his release? But it is right that they should be prepared to take any risk.

Vocabulary

Nouns

οὐσία, ἡ	property
συκοφάντης, ὁ	See below

Adjective

συχνός	much, a great deal of

Verbs

ἀναγκάζειν	compel
ἀπο-βάλλειν	throw away, forfeit, lose
ἐᾶν	allow, permit

Preposition

πρός	+ dative: in addition to, on top of

Aids to comprehension

44e1

μὲν δή is commonly used to close a topic of conversation: "well then, right then". ἐχέτω: "let..." third person imperative (cf. on 43d7-8); singular after neuter plural subject.

e2 ἆρά γε μή: "You're surely not, are you ...?" . ἆρα μή expects a negative reply (an alternative interpretation makes the question more bland: "Can it be the case that ...?"), as ἆρ᾽ οὐ forecasts an affirmative response (cf. 47c3).

e2-3 προμηθῇ ... μή: "show regard/ feel concern on *my* behalf [ἐμοῦ emphatic form] ..., afraid that ..." (then subjunctive to express prospective fear: *MS* D.5).

e3 ἐὰν ... ἐξέλθῃς: Prospective conditional, *MS* D.2, cf. ἐὰν δέῃ at 45a2-3 below.

συκοφάνται: Professional informers/ prosecutors; the term is also used generally of those who abuse the law and the courts for profit and advantage.

e4 πράγματα παρέχωσιν: "provide one [dative] with πράγματα" means "cause one trouble (the "trouble" often having to do with litigation)"; πράγματα ἔχειν, "have bother".

ὡς ... ἐκκλέψασιν: A dative aorist participle, with ἡμῖν; ὡς gives the alleged reason for the proposed litigation: "on the grounds that we ..."

e5 ἀναγκασθῶμεν: First person plural aorist subjunctive passive.

e5-6 ἢ καὶ ... ἢ καί: The first καί strengthens πᾶσαν, "absolutely all"; the second similarly means "even" <something else, more frightful still>.

τι ... παθεῖν: Cf. our euphemistic "If something should happen to me".

45a1

ἔασον [aorist imperative] .. χαίρειν: "allow it to rejoice" (but recall too χαῖρε, "farewell") is an idiomatic way of saying "just disregard, dismiss it, forget about it"; so at 46d7.

a1-2 που: See on 44a2-3.

δίκαιοί ἐσμεν ...: "We are right ..." is best represented in English with an impersonal "it is right that we in rescuing you should run this risk".

a3 δέῃ: Subjunctive of δεῖ.

μείζω: One of the two forms of the accusative singular of the μείζων type, the other being μείζονα.

μὴ ἄλλως ποίει: "don't act otherwise" is a regular way of saying "do just as I say", "don't say no".

45a6-c5

Crito has the necessary money; alternatively, there are others from places other than Athens itself ready to pay. Exile will not be so bad: Thebes would give him a warm welcome.

Vocabulary
Nouns

ἀσφάλεια, ἡ	safety, security
ἀργύριον, τό	(sum of) money
δικαστήριον, τό	court of law

Adjectives

δυσχερής	troublesome, causing difficulty
εὐτελής	cheap

Verbs

κομίζειν	bring
ὑπ-άρχειν	be at (someone's: dative) disposal
κήδεσθαι	care about, concern oneself with the welfare of (genitive)
ἀγαπᾶν	welcome warmly
λυπεῖν	annoy, cause (somebody) trouble

Adverb

ἔπειτα	then, subsequently; next, in the second place, furthermore

Aids to comprehension
45a6

μήτε: "neither": there is no "nor" (a straightforward μή is found as a variant reading), as Crito goes off in another direction; but he gets back on course in b6-7.

καὶ γάρ: "because in point of fact".

οὐδέ: "not even" or "not actually".

a7-8 τἀργύριον: τὸ ἀργύριον, an instance of crasis (ἡ κρᾶσις, "coalescing"); another shortly at b3, = τὰ ἐμά.

θέλουσι for ἐθέλουσι.

ἐξ-αγαγεῖν: Aorist infinitive of ἐξάγειν, tense ἐξ-ήγαγον.

a8-9 τούτους ...: In translation these accusatives should not be sucked into the ὡς clause ["... see how ... these ..."]: "these ..., don't you see how [cf. note on 43b4-5] cheap <they are>?"

καὶ ...: We must supply a "that", an ellipse made easier by the fact that ὡς can mean precisely this, even if it bears a different sense here.

δέοι: Here δεῖ + *genitive* means "there is need of".

ἐπ': "for", "to settle/ fix" them.

45b1-2

σοὶ δὲ ...: "but as for you, you have at your disposal *my* money ..." Singular verb with neuter plural subject.

μέν: Answered by ἔπειτα.

ὡς ... ἱκανά together.

b2 τι: Adverbial, "out of some deep concern for".

b3 ξένοι (so exempt from the attentions of Athenian συκοφάνται) οὗτοι ...: "<there are> foreigners (people not from Athens), the[se] ones <you know about, who visit you every day> here <in the city>".

b4 καί: "actually".

κεκόμικεν: Perfect: see *MS* A.3.a.

ἐπ' αὐτὸ τοῦτο: "for this very purpose".

b4-5 Σιμμίας ... Κέβης: Pythagoreans, they play a prominent part in *Phaedo*.

b6-7 ὥστε: Here, as often, just "so, hence".

ὅπερ: Translate "as".

ἀποκάμῃς: Second person singular aorist subjunctive (after μή-τε, in prohibition: cf. *MS* D.6) of ἀπο-κάμνειν, "flag" (so as to), "relax your efforts" to.

ὃ ἔλεγες ...: See *Apology* 37c4ff.

b8-c1 γενέσθω: "let it prove" third singular aorist imperative (cf. on 43d7-8).

οὐκ ἂν ... σαυτῷ: Literally "you would not have <the knowledge> in what way you should use yourself", i.e. "you wouldn't know what to do with yourself". χρῷο is second person singular optative of χρῆσθαι. The subordinate verb in such a sentence as "I've no idea how to occupy myself" would normally be expressed by the ("deliberative") subjunctive (see *MS* D.6(iv)); the optative here, because the principal verb is itself in the optative ("assimilation"), cf. *MS* E.3.

ἐξελθών: "if you went out <of the country>", into exile.

45c1-2

πολλαχοῦ ...: "in many other places"; ἄλλοσε "to other places" (cf. 51d8, 52b6) rather than ἄλλοθι "in other places" by attraction to the following ὅποι "whither".

ὅποι ἂν ἀφίκῃ: Indefinite clause, *MS* D.3.

c2-3 ἐὰν .. βούλῃ: Prospective conditional, *MS* D.2.

εἰσὶν ἐμοί: "*I* have": he has just talked about *other* possible benefactors.

περὶ πολλοῦ ποιήσονται: See on 44c3.

45c6-46a

In refusing to escape Socrates will gratify his enemies, leave his own sons in the lurch, and lay his associates as well as himself open to the charge of cowardice. He must do as Crito says, and act at once.

Vocabulary

Nouns

ἀνανδρία, ἡ	unmanliness, cowardice
κακία, ἡ	baseness, cowardice
ὥρα, ἡ	(the) time (to ..., infinitive).
ἐχθρός, ὁ	personal enemy

Adjectives

ῥᾴθυμος	lazy, indifferent, carefree, easy
τελευταῖος	final

Verbs

(ἐκ)παιδεύειν	educate
(ἐκ)τρέφειν	rear
σπεύδειν	be anxious, keen, strive
φάσκειν	allege, assert, claim
ἐπι-χειρεῖν	take in hand, undertake
ἐπι-μελεῖσθαι	take care of, care for, cultivate (genitive)
εἰωθέναι	[cf. *MS* A.3.b] be accustomed (to, infinitive), in the habit of ...
προ-διδόναι	betray

Adverb

οὐδαμῶς	in no way, by no means; oblique form μηδαμῶς

Aids to comprehension

45c6-7

ἔτι: See on 44b9-10.

οὐδὲ δίκαιόν ... πρᾶγμα: i.e <irrespective of the question of what people might think> the actual course you are undertaking [viz. σαυτὸν προδοῦναι, "that of -ing ..."] is not right either, it seems to me.

ἐξόν: Impersonal verb (ἔξεστι), so *accusative* absolute , "when it is open to you"; more presently at 45d1, e4, 46a2.

c7-8 τοιαῦτα ... γενέσθαι: "you are keen that ... happen/ be done (in relation) to yourself".

c10 ὑεῖς: There were three of them.

45d2

οἰχήσῃ καταλιπών: "you'll be off [οἴχεσθαι often bears the sense "be gone <from this world>"] and leave them behind".

d2-3 τὸ σὸν μέρος: Accusative of respect, "in relation to your part <in the proceedings>", i.e. "for your part", "as far as you're concerned".

PLATO *CRITO*

ὅτι ἂν ... πράξουσιν: See on 44d9-10; πράττειν here means "fare", and the sense is "they will <just> have to get along as chance directs, take their chance".

d3 τεύξονται: Future of τυγχάνειν, with genitive in the sense "achieve, get, encounter".

ὡς τὸ εἰκός (form: *MS* A.3.b): "as <is> the probability", i.e. "in all probability".

οἷά-: See on 44b8-9.

d4 εἴωθεν: Singular verb after neuter plural.

ἐν ... ὀρφανούς: Crito really piles on the pressure: "in the case of orphans in their orphaned states".

d5 ποιεῖσθαι παῖδας: The term for "begetting children" is παιδοποιεῖσθαι.

²συν-¹δια-ταλαιπωρεῖν: to undergo troubles (all the hard work and heartache involved in the father-son relationship) ¹ through to the end // ² in partnership with them.

d8-9 φάσκοντα: Governed by χρή above, and to be taken in conjunction with διὰ ... βίου: "necessary <for one> anyhow [γε] who has of course/ to be sure [δή] been [cf. on πάλαι at 43b4-5] ..."

ἀρετῆς ... ἐπιμελεῖσθαι: A Socratic principle mentioned frequently in various guises, cf. the pronouncements on ψυχῆς ἐπιμέλεια in *Apology* 29e6ff.

d9 ὡς: "because".

45e1

μή "in the fear that": see on 44e2-3.

e2 τινὶ τῇ ἡμετέρᾳ: "some sort of / degree of ... on our part".

πεπρᾶχθαι: See on 44c8-9.

e3-4 καὶ ... ὡς ... καὶ ... ὡς ...: "<viz.> both the way in which ... and the way in which ..."

ἡ εἴσοδος ... εἰσελθεῖν: Literally "the entering-in of the case into the court, how it [the case] came in [the verb is a technical one for a lawsuit being "brought to court"], when it was possible <for it> not to have come in", i.e. "how the case was brought into court when it need not have been" (Socrates might have left Athens). Cf. *Apology* 29c2ff.

αὐτός ... ἐγένετο: "how the actual legal action was conducted".

e5-6 τὸ τελευταῖον ... πράξεως: τὸ τελευταῖον is (like τὸ νῦν etc.) adverbial (probably); κατάγελως (ὁ), with genitive specifying the target, literally means something that brings mockery on the affair, makes it laughable or ludicrous (cf. adj. καταγέλαστος 53a7). "And last of all, to be sure [δή ironic, as often], this present (-ί) circumstance, which turns the affair into a complete farce, you might say".

e6-46a1 διαπεφευγέναι [perfect infinitive: *MS* A.3.a] ἡμᾶς δοκεῖν: The construction has been explained in various ways: possibly (τουτί, viz.) "that <you> should be thought to have given us the slip", or "that it should be thought

36

that <this business: cf. πρᾶγμα above> has ...", i.e. that we have failed to seize the opportunity to get you out.

46a1

οἵτινες: "seeing that we ...". The relative is causal, as the plain ὅς is commonly (cf. on 44b9-10).

οὐδέ: "and <seeing that> ... <did> not <save> ..."

a2-3 οἷόν τε .. καὶ δυνατόν: "feasible and practicable".

εἴ ... ἦν: ὄφελος is "something of use/ service", "source of help/ advantage". "If there was even some small use of [in] us", i.e "if we had been of the slightest use". A similar expression below, 54a10-b1.

a3 ὅρα μή + subjunctive (cf. *MS* D.5): "see/ watch that ... not".

ἅμα τῷ κακῷ: "along with the κακόν" means "in addition to being a κακόν".

a4 ἀλλά: See on 44b6-7.

μᾶλλον δέ: We say "or rather": cf. 49e5.

a5 βεβουλεῦσθαι: Perfect: *MS* A.4.

a6 τῆς .. ἐπιούσης νυκτός: See on 44a5-6. Crito simply disregards the different scenario suggested by Socrates' dream.

πεπρᾶχθαι: See on 44c8-9.

a6-7 εἰ ... περιμενοῦμεν (future of μένειν: μενεῖν): εἰ + future rather than ἐάν + subjunctive because of the element of urgency or (cf. 47d3-4, 52a4) threat: "if we are going to wait about ..."

a8-9 μηδαμῶς ...: See on 45a3.

46b-47a11

The "power of the many", Socrates argues, may be intimidating, but must be resisted. What opinions, and whose opinions, are worthy of regard?

Vocabulary
Nouns

παιδιά, ἡ	(childish) fun, puerility
προθυμία, ἡ	earnest desire, zealous pursuit (of a goal)
φλυαρία, ἡ	silly talk, nonsense
δεσμός, ὁ	bond(age), imprisonment
Adjectives	
ἀλλοῖος	of another kind, different
κοινός	shared in common; adverb κοινῇ jointly
μέτριος	moderate, reasonable, fair
πονηρός, *opp.* χρηστός	bad: good

PLATO *CRITO*

Verbs

ἀνα-λαμβάνειν	take up, resume
ἐκ-βάλλειν	throw out/ overboard, jettison
ἐπι-πέμπειν	send upon, inflict on, visit with
ἐπι-σκοπεῖν	(with aorist ἐπισκέψασθαι) examine, pursue an inquiry
συγ-χωρεῖν	(with dative) combine with, come to an agreement with, assent to

Adverbs

ἄλλως	idly, to no purpose
ἑκάστοτε	on each and every occasion, invariably
ἔμπροσθεν	in the past, on a previous occasion (also, as here, with τό, as τὸ νῦν etc.)

Prepositions

ἐκτός	(+ genitive) outside of, beyond the range of, exempt from
πρός	(+ genitive) in the name of

Particle

οὐκοῦν	well then, so then

Aids to comprehension
46b1-2

πολλοῦ ἀξία: Literally "worth a lot": ironic no doubt, given that Crito has talked of parting with a lot of money.

εἰ ...: Socrates deals tactfully with the problem posed by his friend's earnest desire to secure his safety. There is a switch from factual to hypothetical (cf. *MS* E.2): " ... <is> ... — if <that is> it were to be accompanied by any rightness", i.e. if there were reason to think that it were also right in any way (τινος: the question is, in theory at least, still open). ὀρθότης-ητος: adj. ὀρθός means "(standing) upright", hence "right, proper, correct".

b2-3 εἰ δὲ μή ...: i.e. should this not prove to be the case, the greater this earnest desire (προθυμία also carries the suggestion of unselfish commitment to someone's cause: often "kindness, selfless devotion" and the like) to implement the proposed course of action the more problematic (for the recipient of these kind attentions) it is.

ὅσῳ ... τοσούτῳ: Literally "by as much as <it is> [ὅσος is a *quantitative relative:* cf. 46e3, 51a5, 53b6, and contrast note on οἷος at 44b8-9] ... by so much <it is> ..."

b3-4 ταῦτα πρακτέον: On the verbal adjective see *MS* B; here it governs the accusative ταῦτα.

b4-5 ὡς: "seeing that", "given that".

38

οὐ νῦν πρῶτον: "... all the MSS and Eusebius [who cites the passage] have οὐ μόνον νῦν. The reading in the text has been restored from a bust of Socrates, in which this sentence has been inscribed as a motto ... the archetype would write οὐ νῦν α for οὐ νῦν πρῶτον. The α would easily be lost before ἀλλά, and the insertion of μόνον would be almost inevitable" (J. Burnet).

τοιοῦτος οἷος: with infinitive: "the sort of person to" (analogous to an infinitival result clause, hence oblique negative μηδενί); supply "I am": cf. on 43d7-8.

τῶν ἐμῶν: The vagueness of this expression can be reproduced with something like "nothing else in my command".

b5-6 λόγῳ: The particular line or mode of argument on a given topic based on the process of reasoning (τὸ λογίζεσθαι), a principle arrived at by logical methods.

ὅς ἄν ... φαίνηται: Indefinite clause, see *MS* D.3.

b6 δή: "be assured", "you may be sure".

b8 γέγονεν: Perfect of γίγνεσθαι, *MS* A.3.a.

σχεδόν τι: τι is often (so too at 53b3) latched on to σχεδόν in the sense of "pretty well, just about".

46c1

πρεσβεύω: A high-sounding word, to express the notion of giving primacy to someone or something that is an object of reverence.

c2-3 ὧν: Relative serving as sentence-connective; genitive of comparison, cf. shortly c3-4.

ἐὰν μή ...: Prospective conditional, *MS* D.2.

βελτίω: Neuter plural of βελτίων, alternatively βελτίονα (cf. the note on 45a3).

ἐν τῷ παρόντι: A neuter participle, "in our present situation", or "at the present time".

c3 οὐ μή .. συγχωρήσω: (aorist subjunctive: cf. *MS* D.6) See on 44b8-9.

c3-5 οὐδ' ἄν ... μορμολύττηται: ἄν [α] for ἐάν (cf. on 44d4-5, and *MS* D.2); πλείω (see above on 46c2-3, βελτίω), from πολύς, is an accusative of respect; the expressive verb μορμολύττεσθαι means "scare", "terrify", "put the frighteners on", with the threat of Μορμώ, a bogey-name used for frightening children. "... not even if ... scares us in relation to more things than the present ones", i.e. with even more terrors than those which confront us at the present time.

c6 ἀφαιρέσεις: "takings-away" (ἀφαιρεῖν -εῖσθαι), "confiscations".

c7 αὐτά: See on 44c8-9.

εἰ: "suppose" we were to ..., cf. *MS* E.2.

c8 πότερον, "whether", often (cf. 47b1, c11 etc.) prefaces the first of two alternative propositions in a *direct* question; redundant in English.

39

46d2

πρὶν .. ἐμὲ δεῖν: πρίν with accusative (to mark change of subject) and infinitive, "before x happens/ happened".

d3-4 νῦν ... ἐγένετο: "whereas now it has been made/ turned out to be crystal-clear [κατα- is intensive] after all [ἄρα: cf. on 49a9, 50e7-9]".

ἕνεκα λόγου: "for the sake of talking", "<just> for argument's sake".

d4-5 ὡς ἀληθῶς: ὡς, "in such and such a fashion", simply anticipates the following adverbial suffix: "in a true way", "really and truly", "in reality".

d5-6 κοινῇ μετὰ σοῦ: There are many references in Plato (and in Xenophon) to Socrates' habit of examining a question "jointly": cf. below, 48d9.

d6 ἀλλοιότερος: The comparative here has its so-called "contrasting" function, not "more different" but "different, rather <than the same>".

d7 ἐάσομεν χαίρειν: Before this supply "whether" from immediately above; see on 45a1.

πεισόμεθα: See on 47c3.

d8-9 πως: "somehow", "in some way", looks forward to ὧδε: "in some such way as this".

τῶν ... λέγειν: "by those <among us> who considered they were saying something", i.e. were speaking to the point, knew what they were talking about. Ctr. οὐδὲν λέγειν (note on 47d6).

νυνδή: "just now", "a moment ago".

46e1

δοξάζουσιν: i.e. *entertain* opinions; like μάχην μάχεσθαι, νίκην νικᾶν and so on.

δέοι: Optative of δεῖ, deployed in indirect speech, past sequence (cf. *MS* E.3).

περὶ πολλοῦ ποιεῖσθαι: See on 44c3.

e2 τοῦτο: Emphatically placed.

e3 ὅσα γε τἀνθρώπεια (i.e. τὰ ἀνθρ-, crasis): ὅσον and ὅσα, "as much/ many as" (cf. on 46b2-3) often bear a restrictive sense, "as far as x <goes, is concerned>"; so here "as far anyway as human affairs go" means "as far as one can forecast anyway given the human condition", where death can in any given case strike suddenly and without warning. Cf. 54d6-7, "as far as *my* present beliefs go at any rate".

τοῦ μέλλειν: Articular infinitive, see *MS* C.3, 5.

47a1

αὔριον: Crito believes that the ship will arrive today, and that Socrates will have to die tomorrow. Socrates here simply takes the side of his sceptical interlocutor.

παρακρούοι: παρα-κρούειν, "strike out of true", probably alludes to mental derangement (so παρακόπτειν commonly). We might translate "grossly distort/ skew your judgement/ powers of reasoning".

a2 δή + imperative (very common indeed) can be represented by (depending on context) "now", "come now", "then", "just".

a11 πῶς δ᾽ οὔ; This, and πῶς γὰρ οὔ;, are regularly used to express instant assent: "and/ for how not?" i.e. "surely", "of course".

47a12-d7

The only opinion worth considering is that of the single expert in a given field — morality included. Otherwise the body or that part of us [i.e. the soul] which is made better by right and destroyed by wrong, as the case may be, will be ruined.

Vocabulary

Nouns

ἔπαινος, ὁ	praise, commendation
ψόγος, ὁ	adverse criticism, censure

Adjective

σύμ-πας	in plur., all together

Verbs

ἀτιμάζειν	dishonour, show no respect for
ἐπ-αΐειν	be an expert
ἀσπάζεσθαι	greet warmly, welcome
γυμνάζεσθαι	train as a gymnast/ athlete
ἕπεσθαι	(with dative) follow, comply with
ἀκολουθεῖν	(with dative) follow
ἀπειθεῖν	(with dative) disobey, refuse to comply with
δι-ιέναι (διέρχομαι)	go through, enumerate

Particle

εἶεν	(used in argument) well now, right then

Aids to comprehension
47a12

φέρε: Like ἄγε, "come".
δή: See on 47a2.
αὖ: "again", as we turn to a fresh former topic of conversation.
τὰ τοιαῦτα: "such cases <as the following>".

47b1

καὶ τοῦτο πράττων: "and who makes this his business [πρᾶγμα, "occupation"]" — as a professional athlete.

πότερον: See on 46c8.

b3 ὃς ἂν τυγχάνῃ: Indefinite clause, another at 47b10: *MS* D.3; τυγχ. ὤν, "he happens to be", would do; better perhaps (so quite often; cf. 49b5, 52a8) "he really is", "is in fact": "... is his actual doctor ..."

παιδοτρίβης: "his trainer". — For the functions of doctor and trainer see *Gorgias* 452a6ff. (cf. also id. 464a1ff.).

b6 ἀλλὰ μή: English prefers "and not" in such antitheses.

b8 δῆλα δή: "quite obviously"; sometimes written δηλαδή. Contrast 48b1, and compare the note on 53a5.

b9-10 ταύτῃ: Emphatic: "It is in this way ..., <viz.> in whatever way [ἧ ἂν: cf. *MS* D.3] ..."

ἄρα: Inferentially, "then".

πρακτέον ... ποτέον: On this clutch of verbal adjectives see *MS* B; αὐτῷ dative of agent, "by him".

καὶ (ἑδ.) γε: "yes, and ...", these last two verbal adjectives referring specifically to the regimen prescribed by the physician.

b10 ἐπιστάτῃ: An ἐπι-στάτης is someone who stands over (ἐφ-ίστασθαι), a supervisor; but a connection with ἐπίστασθαι, "to know, be in the know, possess (specialised) knowledge", is clearly felt: cf. the ensuing participial expression.

b12 ἔστι ταῦτα: See on 43c4.

47c2

τοὺς τῶν πολλῶν: Supply ἐπαίνους.

c3 μηδέν: A class or category, not a set of specific individuals, hence μη- not οὐ.

ἆρα οὐ-: See on 44e2.

πείσεται: This time (ctr. 44c4, 46d7; and 48e1) future of πάσχειν, not of πείθεσθαι.

c4 πῶς γὰρ οὔ; See on 47a11.

c5-6 ἔστι: Note the accent: "is actually".

ποῖ τείνει: Literally "in what direction does it tend?" (τείνειν "stretch", used intransitively, "stretch out, extend, reach", hence often "be relevant to", "concern"); amplified by εἰς τί τῶν ..., "into what of the things belonging to the person who ...?", i.e. "into what part of the person who ...?"

c7 τοῦτο: Emphatic: "this is what ..."

δι- in such compounds means, if it means anything at all, "completely".

c8-9 τἆλλα: Crasis, τὰ ἄλλα; accusative of relation, "in respect of all other areas".

οὕτως: Supply ἔχει, "is it the case".

c9 ἵνα ...: Purpose clause, *MS* D.4.

διῑωμεν: See *MS* D.7.

καὶ δὴ καί: This run is used predominantly as a vehicle for passing from the general (in this case τἆλλα) to the subject of immediate interest: "and in particular/ specifically" in relation to ...

c11 πότερον: Best taken as the start of a fresh sentence; see on 46c8.

47d3-4

ᾧ: Cf. on 46c2-3.

εἰ μή + future: see on 46a6-7.

d4 λωβησόμεθα: λωβᾶσθαι is a strong word: to inflict λώβη, outrageous physical maltreatment, including maiming and mutilation, on.

d5 ἐγίγνετο ... ἀπώλλυτο: Imperfect, referring to the *previous* discussions, in the course of which these and similar things ἐλέγετο; "is made <as we argued> ..."

d6 οὐδέν: Cf. our idiom "there is nothing in what you say"; οὐδὲν λέγειν = speak irrelevantly, talk rot.

47d8-48b9

With our body or that other part of our makeup destroyed is life worth living? No, the opinion of the many can be disregarded. The many can put us to death, true: but what matters is not "living", but "living well", to be defined as "living commendably and justly".

Vocabulary

Adjectives

ἐναντίος	opposite
θαυμάσιος	admirable, admired
τίμιος	valuable
ὑγιεινός	conducive to health, healthy, salubrious
φαῦλος	poor in quality/ value; in comparative, of lesser value or significance
νοσώδης	inducing ill health, insalubrious

Verb

ὀνινάναι	benefit

Aids to comprehension
47d8

φέρε δή: As 47a12.

ἐάν clause: *MS* D.2.

d10-e1 πειθόμενοι μὴ ...: "by adhering to what is *not* the opinion of ... <but instead to that of οἱ πολλοί>".

βιωτόν: "to be lived", i.e. "is our life worth living?"

διεφθαρμένου: Perfect participle passive (*MS* A.5) of δια-φθείρειν; genitive absolute.

47e1-2

που expresses varying degrees of certainty or self-assurance in the posing of questions: "surely", "one may presume", "perhaps".

σῶμα is the predicate: "this <element> is <to be identified as> 'body'".

e4 μοχθηροῦ (μόχθος "distress", "a painful, debilitating condition"): "afflicted", "in sorry physical shape".

e6 οὐδαμῶς: For the point cf. *Gorgias* 512a2ff., *Republic* 445a5ff.

e7 ἀλλὰ ... διεφθαρμένου: Note the word-order: μετ᾽ ἐκείνου carries great emphasis.

ἄρ᾽: Cf. note on 47b9-10; below, 48a5.

e8 ὅ: A variant reading ᾧ has generally been preferred (a plausible case could be made for either): with that, λωβᾶσθαι will govern the dative, and a ὅ is to be understood as the object of ὀνίνησιν (there is no problem with this).

e9-48a1 τοῦ σώματος: Genitive of comparison.

ἐκεῖνο ... ἐστίν: Literally, "that thing, whatever on earth (ποτε) it is [the *indicative* is normal in parenthetic relative clauses of this kind: cf. 50a7] of what we possess, around which are ...", i.e. that part, whatever precise part of us this is, the part that is the province of ...

ἐστίν: The antonyms may be conceptualised as a single whole, hence the number of this verb.

48a4

πολύ γε: "Yes, much/ far <more>"; see on 43b8-9.

a5 οὐκ ... πάνυ: οὐ πάνυ often means "not by any means" rather than "not quite".

ἡμῖν .. φροντιστέον: Verbal adjective: *MS* B; ἡμῖν dative of agent.

οὕτω: "under these circumstances", given what has been established.

a6 ἐροῦσιν: From ἐρεῖν future of λέγειν.

ἡμᾶς: "of, about us".

a7-8 ὥστε: See on 45b6-7.

πρῶτον μέν: There is no "and in the second place": with ἀλλὰ μὲν δή at a10 Socrates switches from what Crito has said to a possible counterargument put forward by τις. Cf. 50d1-2, 53b3; 50e3.

εἰσηγῇ ...: εἰσηγεῖσθαι = put forward a proposal or motion, to the effect that [infinitive] ...

a10 ἀλλὰ μὲν δή = ἀλλὰ μέντοι, "but still", "but despite what you say".

a11 γ': Best taken closely with φαίη .. ἄν: "might well say".
ἀποκτεινύναι for -κτείνειν.

48b1
φαίη γὰρ ἄν expresses agreement with Socrates' φαίη γ' ἄν τις.

b2-4 ἀληθῆ λέγεις sounds pretty flat here, to say the least. It is perhaps better put into Crito's mouth: he is certainly in assenting mood by this stage. But critics have argued long and hard about what to do with the three components of the sequence δῆλα ... λέγεις.

ὦ θαυμάσιε: This adjective can be used ironically, and sometimes it carries the suggestion of "extraordinary", "weird and wonderful", "bizarre". In that respect this mode of address has something in common with others in Plato and elsewhere, and especially with ὦ δαιμόνιε, cf. on 44b6-7.

τε should look forward to "καὶ this other..."; with καὶ τόνδε δὲ αὖ ... (supply λόγον, "but consider this <argument> as well in its turn") strict coordination is jettisoned.

δι-εληλύθαμεν: First person plural perfect (*MS* A.3.a) of δι-έρχομαι.

ἔτι ὅμοιος .. καὶ πρότερον: καί means "as", cf. Latin *similis ac/ atque:* "still much the same as before".

b4-5 μένει: "remains <as it stood>", i.e. "holds good".

τὸ ζῆν: Articular infinitive, cf. *MS* C.3-4.

περὶ πλείστου ποιητέον: See on 44c3; verbal adjective: *MS* B.

... ἀλλὰ τὸ εὖ ζῆν: Cf. *Apology* 28b2ff. (and *Gorgias* 512d8ff.).

b6 ἀλλά counters any suggestion that the proposition may *not* hold good: "But of course it does". Cf. on 49e4.

b7 δικαίως: Picked up by the question πότερον δίκαιον κτλ. b11.

ταὐτόν: Crasis, for τὸ αὐτόν (alternative form αὐτό).

48b10-49a3

Socrates: "Is it right or not right for me to escape? That is the question to be addressed: nothing else matters".

Vocabulary
Nouns

ἡσυχία, ἡ	tranquillity, quiet; -ίαν ἄγειν keep quiet; lie low, remain inactive
τροφή, ἡ	rearing, upbringing
ἀνάλωσις, ἡ	spending, expenditure
σκέψις, ἡ ~ σκέμμα-ατος, τό	matter for reflection or discussion, inquiry; consideration

Verbs

ἀντι-λέγειν	speak in opposition, offer a counterargument
παρα-μένειν	stand one's ground, stand fast
ἀπο-κρίνεσθαι	answer
ὁμολογεῖν	agree upon, admit, concede in argument
τελεῖν	pay
ἀφ-ιέναι	let go, set free

Aids to comprehension

48b10

ἐκ: "on the basis of", "following on from".

σκεπτέον: *MS* B.

b11-c1 μὴ ἀφιέντων Ἀθηναίων: Genitive absolute, μή because there is a condition implicit in the participle. Note the absence of the definite article with the name, with reference to Athenians as a corporate body. We might translate "without the city's consenting to my release".

48c1-2

ἐάν clause: *MS* D.2. Note the switch to εἰ, εἰ δὲ μή being the normal way of saying "otherwise".

πειρώμεθα ... ἐῶμεν: Subjunctives to express "let us" (*MS* D.6(i)), cf. below d9.

ἐῶμεν: "let <it> be, forget <it>".

c2-3 ἅς ... σκέψεις: "But as for the considerations you mention", a relative clause whose antecedent is swallowed up within it; picked up presently by ταῦτα ... σκέμματα ᾖ.

c4-5 μὴ ... ᾖ: μή with the third person subjunctive (*MS* D.6(iii)) is a way of saying "perhaps/ maybe/ it could be that/ I fear that" ... is (is *not*: μὴ οὐ); cf. below c7-8, d3-4. ᾖ singular after neuter plural subject.

ὡς ἀληθῶς: See on 46d4-5.

c5-6 ἀποκτεινύντων for -κτεινόντων cf. on 48a11.

καὶ .. ἄν means "and who, yes, would bring them back to life again [βιώσκεσθαι, "make alive", ἀνά "back again"] <just as ῥᾳδίως>", the participial clause constituting a "conditional apodosis".

c6 οὐδενὶ ξὺν νῷ: ξύν for σύν; the reference to totally irrational, mindless behaviour effectively heralds the contemptuous τούτων, "these ..."

c7-8 ἡμῖν: Dative of agent, with σκεπτέον; emphatically placed, pointing a contrast with the conduct associated with οἱ πολλοί at the close of the previous sentence.

ὁ λόγος οὕτως αἱρεῖ: "the process of reasoning/ reasoned argument so proves/ establishes the validity of the point at issue"; αἱρεῖν, "catch", in a court of law "secure a conviction", "win a case".

c8 νυνδή: See on 46d8-9.

48d1-2

ἐξάξουσιν: Future participle, dative plural: "who will/ are going to ..."

ἐξάγοντές τε καὶ ἐξαγόμενοι: These plurals are used loosely in the wake of "we". He means "and <whether> we ourselves — you the rescuer and I the rescued — <will be acting rightly>".

d2 τῇ ἀληθείᾳ: Dative of manner, "in reality", "really".

d3 κἄν i.e. καὶ ἐάν; on the latter see *MS* D.2.

φαινώμεθα with participle, "we are seen to/ are plainly ..."

d4 ὑπολογίζεσθαι: "take into account" the question whether ...

d5-6 ἄλλο ὁτιοῦν: "anything else whatever": neuter of ὁστισ-οῦν = "anybody whatsoever".

πάσχειν: Supply εἰ δεῖ.

πρὸ τοῦ ἀδικεῖν: πρό is used here in the sense of "in preference to" (cf. 52c8, 54b5): i.e. "sooner/ rather than doing wrong". Articular infinitive: *MS* C.3.

d8 δρῶμεν: Deliberative subjunctive (*MS* D.6(iv)), "we are to do".

d9 κοινῇ: See on 46d5-6.

πῇ: "in any way".

48e1

πείσομαι: See on 47c3.

e2 παῦσαι: Aorist imperative singular middle, "stop".

ἤδη: Here, as frequently, in the sense "right away", "right now".

ὦ μακάριε: See on 44c6-7.

e3 ἀκόντων Ἀθηναίων: Genitive absolute, there being no need for the participle ὤν with either ἄκων-οντος or its opposite ἑκών-όντος: "without the city's consent" (cf. on 48b11-c1).

e3-5 ὡς: "because".

περὶ πολλοῦ ποιοῦμαι: See on 44c3; here with infinitive, "think it very important, attach much importance" to ...

πείσας σε ... ἀλλὰ μὴ ἄκοντος (supply σοῦ): "having persuaded you, but not [see however note on 47b6] with your being [cf. on 48e3 above] reluctant", i.e. "with your consent rather than against your wishes".

e5 δή strengthens the imperative (cf. on 47a2): "Look, won't you, at ..."

τὴν ἀρχήν: "the starting-point", "initial principle/ assumption".

ἐάν (see *MS* D.2): "to see if ..."

49a1-2

ᾗ ἂν ...: Indefinite clause with subjunctive (*MS* D.3), "in whatever manner you think most <apt>/ best".

a3 ἀλλά expressing consent (cf. on 43d7-8), "well", "very well".

πειράσομαι: Note the irregular -ασ-.

49a4-e8

Crito has to admit that one should not under any circumstances commit a wrong or inflict injury, or act thus in retaliation; and that an undertaking — an undertaking with right on its side — should be honoured.

Vocabulary

Noun

ὁμολογία, ἡ	agreement, point agreed upon, admission

Verbs

δια-φέρειν	(with genitive) differ from
ἐμ-μένειν	(with dative) stand by, hold to
ἀμύνεσθαι	defend oneself
δια-λέγεσθαι	converse, engage in dialogue
κακουργεῖν	see below
κατα-φρονεῖν	(with genitive) despise, regard with contempt
κοινωνεῖν	share (a belief); also with genitive

Adverbs

ἐντεῦθεν	hence, from this point
πρόσθε(ν)	formerly, on earlier occasions
σπουδῇ	earnestly, seriously

Aids to comprehension
49a4ff.

Discussion revolves around the following key terms: ἀδικεῖν act unjustly, do wrong, wrong someone; κακουργεῖν work evil, often used of physical maltreatment or injury; κακῶς ποιεῖν do (one, accusative) badly i.e. treat badly, maltreat ~ κακῶς πάσχειν i.e. be treated badly, be maltreated. The act of retaliation is expressed by the preverb ἀντι-, thus: ἀνταδικεῖν, ἀντικακουργεῖν [these two later also: 54c2-3], and also ἀντιδρᾶν κακῶς (treat badly, maltreat ...); cf. ἀντιποιεῖν (50e7, e9), ἀντιτύπτειν (51a1-2), ἀνταπολλύναι (51a6).

a4 ... ἑκόντας ἀδικητέον εἶναι: "that one ought to ... intentionally", a natural use of the accusative since ἀδικητέον εἶναι (see *MS* B.4) may be thought of as the equivalent of ἀδικεῖν δεῖν.

a5ff. For this whole sequence the following passages from *Gorgias* are worth comparing: 469b1ff., 474c5ff., 508e4ff.

a5-6 τό γε ἀδικεῖν: Articular infinitive (cf. *MS* C.2-3), "actual wrongdoing".

ἡμῖν: "by us", cf. a7, b2.

[**a7** ὅπερ καὶ ἄρτι ἐλέγετο is intrusive: it must relate to αἱ πρόσθεν ὁμολογίαι, i.e. "a point made recently <in 46b6-7>".]

a8-9 ἐκκεχυμέναι εἰσίν serves as the third person plural perfect passive (*MS* A.5) of ἐκ-χέω, "have been poured out/ away", "thrown overboard/ down the drain".

a9 ἄρα: Here a disillusioned "after all", "it turns out in retrospect".

τηλικοίδε (singular -όσδε): "at our <advanced> age", cf. τηλικοῦτοι at 43c1.

[γέροντες: The word spells out what is meant by τηλικοίδε ἄνδρες and is clearly intrusive.]

a10-b1 ... ἐλάθομεν ...: λανθάνειν with reflexive + participle, "escape the detection of oneself doing": transl. "... have we all this time been conversing [πάλαι: see on 43b4-5] without noticing that we're no different ...?".

49b1

παντὸς μᾶλλον: "more than anything", i.e. "most definitely", "incontrovertibly".

b3-4 εἴτε καὶ πραότερα: "or if you like/ for that matter milder things", an example of a "polar" expression: the opposite of case or situation *x* is appended for purposes of intensification or emphasis.

b5 τυγχάνει ὄν: "is in fact", see on 47b3.

φαμὲν ἢ οὔ; φάναι "say yes" (cf. 44a4), οὐ φάναι "say no": so "yes or no?".

b7 ἄρα: See on 47b9-10; cf. b9, c10.

b8 οὐ δῆτα: "no indeed"; οὐ .. δήπου in c3 is scarcely less positive.

b9-10 οὐδὲ ...: Supply δεῖ.

ὡς ... οἴονται: "But I do have one good skill,/ that's to repay whoever hurts me with a/ corresponding ill" wrote Archilochus in the 7th century (transl. M.L. West). A doctrine deeply rooted in Greek morality.

ἐπειδή γε: "because of course ..."; we are dealing with a point that has just been established.

49c2

τί δὲ δή; provides an animated lead-in to a fresh point: "and what <of this> then?", "a further point/ question then" (cf. τί δέ; shortly at c4).

c7 τὸ ... κακῶς ποιεῖν ἀνθρώπους: Articular infinitive, as is the ensuing τοῦ ἀδικεῖν (see *MS* C.3-5): "the act of doing/ treating people badly, maltreating them".

που: "presumably".

c11 οὐδ' ἂν ὁτιοῦν πάσχῃ: Literally "not even if [ἂν = ἐάν, *MS* D.2] <one> suffers anything whatever [cf. on 48d5-6]", i.e. "no matter what treatment one receives".

c11-d1 ὅρα ... ὅπως μή with subjunctive (*MS* D.5), "watch that you don't ..."

ταῦτα καθομολογῶν: "in yielding these points", the preverb (as notably in κατα-δοκεῖν) implying that the activity is directed against, prejudicial to one(self), viz. παρὰ δόξαν (d1), "contrary to your own belief/ convictions".

49d2

ταῦτα: Neuter plural subject, hence the singular verbs.

d3 δέδοκται: Perfect passive of δοκεῖν, *MS* A.5.

d3-4 κοινὴ βουλή: "a common counsel", i.e. "common ground" as a basis for discussion; then βουλεύματα, "the results of their deliberations/ discussions".

d4 ἀνάγκη: Cf. on 43d5-6.

d5-6 δή with imperative: see on 47a2.

εὖ μάλα: i.e. with the utmost care.

d6 συνδοκεῖ: Literally "it [such a viewpoint] seems right to you jointly-with <me>".

d6-9 ἀρχώμεθα: Deliberative subjunctive in indirect form: *MS* D.6(iv).

ἐντεῦθεν ...: ὡς ... ἔχοντος is a genitive absolute, with the articular infinitives (*MS* C.2-3) τοῦ ἀδικεῖν / τοῦ ἀνταδικεῖν as subjects: literally, "the act of wrongdoing ... never being, it is argued/ assumed (ὡς) ...". With οὔτε κακῶς ... there is a switch to accusative + infinitive, lit. "that one should ..." Translate: "from this point, the argument/ assumption that it is never the right thing either to ... or to ... or, if one is badly treated, to defend oneself by inflicting bad treatment in retaliation".

d9-e1 ἀφίστασαι: Second person singular present of ἀφίστασθαι, "stand apart", i.e. "dissociate yourself".

τῆς ἀρχῆς: Cf. on 48e5.

49e2

πῃ ἄλλῃ: "in some other way".

διδάσκε: As often, "explain", "put in the picture".

e3 τὸ μετὰ τοῦτο: "the point after this", "my next point".

e4 ἀλλ' ἐμμένω turns the possibility fielded by Socrates into a firm statement of fact: "But of course I stand by them" ; cf. on 48b6.

ἀλλὰ λέγε: For this use of the particle see on 44b6-7.

e5 λέγω ... ἐρωτῶ: Literally "Very well [δή responds to the request], I say in turn the thing after this, but rather I ask", i.e. "Very well, my next point — or rather [cf. on 46a4] question — is this".

e6-7 πότερον: See on 46c8.

ἃ ἄν τις ὁμολογήσῃ τῳ: Indefinite clause (*MS* D.3), "whatever things someone has [aorist subjunctive] agreed with somebody [unaccented τῳ = τινι]".

δίκαια ὄντα: An important qualification: "— provided that they are right —".

ποιητέον ἢ ἐξαπατητέον: See *MS* B. Literally "is it necessary to do whatever ..., or is it necessary to practise deceit <on the person in question>?".

49e9-50c4

"Suppose", Socrates continues, "the Laws confronted me and accused me of setting out to destroy them and the city too, how could they be answered?"

Vocabulary
Nouns

ἰδιώτης, ὁ	private individual
ῥήτωρ-ορος, ὁ	public speaker; public advocate (chosen by state to defend laws against proposed changes/ annulment)

Adjectives

κύριος	valid
~ ἄκυρος	invalid

Verbs

ἀπο-διδράσκειν	run away
δικάζειν	give a judgement (δίκας δικάζειν deliver legal judgements or verdicts)
ἰσχύειν	have force
κρίνειν	judge
ὀνομάζειν	name, call, term
προσ-τάττειν	prescribe, direct, stipulate (that ... should, accusative + infinitive)
ἀθρεῖν	observe, consider
ἐν-νοεῖν	understand
ἐπι-χειρεῖν	(with dative) put one's hand to, attempt; (with infinitive) attempt to
δια-νοεῖσθαι	intend
ἐρέσθαι	(an aorist: tense ἠρόμην) ask, question

Aids to comprehension
49e9

ἐκ τούτων δὴ ἄθρει: Note the order: "It is on the basis of *these* considerations then that you must consider <the issue>".

51

e9-50a1 μὴ πείσαντες: Not οὐ π., as we are dealing with a hypothesis.

πότερον: See on 46c8.

50a1-2

καὶ ταῦτα: A common way of saying "and that too": "people ..., and people at that whom ..."

a2-3 οἶς ...: i.e. τούτοις ἅ ... δίκαια ὄντα ("as being ..."), relative attraction (note on 43d3), the participial unit being drawn in as well.

a6 ἀλλ': See on 44b6-7.

εἰ: See *MS* E.2.

μέλλουσιν is dative participle, to be taken with ἡμῖν; governed by (ἐλθόντες καὶ) ἐπιστάντες a couple of lines on.

a7 ὅπως ... τοῦτο "apologises" for the choice of the verb ἀπο-διδράσκειν applied to the speedy exit envisaged by Crito (δραπέτης "runaway", "runaway slave"; cf. 52d1-2 below): "in what way one should term this", i.e. "whatever one cares [cf. on 47e9-48a1] to call it".

a8 τὸ κοινὸν τῆς πόλεως: The state viewed as a corporate entity, there to serve the common interest: "the state-community", "the commonwealth".

ἐπι-στάντες of a sudden confrontation, "having appeared/ presented themselves", as in a dream (ἐ φ-ίστασθαι: participle -στάς -στᾶσα -στάν is used intransitively).

a9 ἄλλο τι ἤ: "something other than" (or just ἄλλο τι) commonly prefaces questions expecting an affirmative reply; transl., e.g., "are you not just/ simply ...?", "you are ... surely!".

50b2

τὸ σὸν μέρος: Cf. on 45d2-3; here the sarcastic "as your contribution to the proceedings" implies "as much as you can get away with", cf. καθ' ὅσον δύνασαι at 51a5.

δοκεῖ σοι in parenthesis, "do you think?", with οἷόν τε supply "is it?".

b3 εἶναι: "exist".

ἀνα-τετράφθαι: Perfect infinitive passive (*MS* A.5) of ἀ να-τρέπειν, "be overturned, capsize".

b3-4 ἐν ᾗ ἂν ...: Indefinite (*MS* D.3), in keeping with the generalised nature of the argumentation: "that city, a city in which ..."

αἱ γενόμεναι δίκαι: "the judgements that have been made/ the decisions that have been arrived at <in the courts>".

b5 ἐροῦμεν: Future of λέγειν.

b7 ἄλλως τε καί: "especially", "above all"; very common indeed.

b7-8 ὑπὲρ ... ἀπολλυμένου: "in defence of this law in the process of (under threat of) being destroyed/ obliterated [an echo of the strong language of 50b1]".

τὰς δίκας τὰς δικασθείσας: The forceful assonance can be reproduced with something along the lines of "those legal decisions that have been legally arrived at".

50c1
ὅτι as often introduces a *direct* quotation.
γάρ: "<Yes, I do propose to take this illegal step>, because ..."
c2 τὴν δίκην: Here "the case".
c4 νὴ Δία: Cf. on 43b3.

50c5-51c5

The Laws: "The agreement was that you would obey us without any qualification, as our child and slave. You must put your fatherland above all else: in putting up any opposition you might try persuasion but not force".

Vocabulary
Nouns

ἔκγονος, ὁ	offspring
πρόγονος, ὁ	forefather, ancestor
τάξις, ἡ	(battle-) post

Adjectives

ἅγιος	sacred
ὅσιος	pious, righteous
σεμνός	august, revered

Verbs

τιτρώσκειν	wound
τύπτειν	strike, hit
ὑπ-είκειν	submit to, give way to
φράζειν	tell, explain
βιάζεσθαι	treat with violence
μέμφεσθαι	(with dative) find fault with, criticise
σέβεσθαι	revere, treat reverentially
ἐγ-καλεῖν	(with dative) bring a charge or accusation against

Adverb

ἴσως	perhaps, maybe

Aids to comprehension
50c5-6
ἄν: i.e. ἐάν, *MS* D.2.

53

ἤ: Cf. on 43a1.

καί: "too", ταῦτα the possibility of questioning the validity of legal decisions; in the ensuing ἤ clause we might insert an "only".

ὡμολόγητο: *Plu*perfect passive (*MS* A.6) of ὁμολογεῖν, singular because the subject is a neuter plural. — Law is regarded as an agreement or contract (ὁμολογία, συνθήκη) between state and individual.

ἡμῖν τε καὶ σοί: Datives expressing the agent; for the order see on 44b9-10.

c6-7 ἐμμενεῖν: *Future* infinitive with ὁμολογεῖν, not present (-μένειν, see on 46a6-7).

αἷς [i.e. ταύταις ἃς, cf. on 43d3] ἂν ...: Indefinite clause, cf. *MS* D.3.

c7 θαυμάζοιμεν with genitive: see on 43b4-5.

c8 ὅτι: See on 50c1.

c9 καί: "in fact".

εἴωθας: See *MS* A.3.b.

c10 τῷ ... ἀποκρίνεσθαι: Articular infinitives (*MS* C.2-3), " the technique of ..." The Socratic method is often described in these terms, cf. e.g. *Phaedo* 72d2-3, *Republic* 534d9-10.

φέρε: See on 47a12.

50d1-2

πρῶτον μέν: No formal correspondence: instead the lively ἀλλά of d5. Cf. on 48a7-8.

d2-3 ἐγεννήσαμεν ... ἐφύτευσεν: γεννᾶν = "generate", "procreate", φυτεύειν = "beget".

ἡμεῖς carries emphasis of course, as does δι' ἡμῶν, "was it not through us that ...?"

d4-5 ὡς with (dative) participle, "on the ground that", i.e. "do you have any criticism of their quality?".

d5 ἀλλά introducing a fresh question after a rejected suggestion, "well".

d7-8 ἦ [not ἤ] οὐ: "Isn't it indeed the case that ...?", cf. on 43a1.

ἐπὶ τούτῳ τεταγμένοι (cf. *MS* A.5): "posted over/ in charge of this", i.e. "assigned to this sphere".

d8-e1 παρ-αγγέλλοντες: "in issuing instructions".

ἐν ... παιδεύειν: i.e. to furnish you with an education that is both cultural and physical. See *Oxford Classical Dictionary*, 3rd ed., pp.506-7.

50e2

ἐξ-ετράφης: Aorist passive of ἐκτρέφειν.

e3-4 πρῶτον μέν: Cf. on 50d1-2 (here taken up with καὶ εἰ ... e4).

καὶ .. καί: "both ... and".

e5 ἐξ ἴσου ... ἡμῖν: ἐξ ἴσου means "on an equal basis". The argument is: in questions of what is "(legally) right", can the individual regard himself as being on a level footing with the law(s)? If he does enjoy equal status, then he can legitimately take retaliatory action if he so chooses.

e6-7 ἅττ᾽ ἂν ...: Indefinite clause, *MS* D.3; ἅττ᾽ = ἅτινα, neuter plural of ὅστις.

ἡμεῖς ... σοί (with δίκαιον εἶναι): Both carry emphasis, the latter reinforced by καί.

σε (.. ποιεῖν:) "to you".

ἀντιποιεῖν: See on 49a4ff.

e7-9 ἢ πρὸς ... ἐτύγχανεν: "Or is it the case that in relation to your father on the one hand right was not on a level footing for you [shared by you on an equal basis], and [another example: we would say "or"] in relation to your master, if you happened to have one ...?"

ἄρα: "after all", "when you reflect on it"; a matching example in the balancing clause of 51a3.

σοι: A dative pronoun equivalent to a possessive is frequently encountered with words denoting family members; still, the force of the pronoun must also be felt with the imminent ἐξ ἴσου.

e9 ἅπερ πάσχοις: Indefinite, optative after past tense ἦν (cf. *MS* E.3), "whatever treatment you received".

51a1-2

οὔτε ... πολλά: This sequence harks back to οὐκ ἐξ ἴσου ἦν τὸ δίκαιον· "<such an equal right was not available to you> so that you could either [put negatively in the Greek, in the wake of οὐ] ... or ..."

κακῶς ἀκούοντα ἀντιλέγειν: "talk back if you were reviled/ run down"; κακῶς ἀκούειν serves as passive of κακῶς λέγειν, "speak badly of, criticise" etc.; cf. 53e3.

a2-3 πρὸς δὲ ... σοι: "while in relation to ... on the other hand it *will* be permissible for you <to indulge in this kind of retaliatory behaviour>?".

a3 ἐάν clause: see *MS* D.2.

a4 καὶ σὺ δέ: This is an example of "δέ in apodosis", coming here, as often, in the wake of a conditional protasis (ἐάν ..., cf. *MS* D.2): the effect is to arrest the attention of the listener, "with this consequence, that if *we* ..., *you* then for your part [καί] ..."

a5 καθ᾽ ὅσον: "as far as"; cf. on 46b2-3.

a7 τῇ ἀληθείᾳ: See on 48d2.

τῆς ἀρετῆς ἐπιμελούμενος: Cf. 45d8-9.

a8 σοφός: "clever".

λέληθέν σε: Perfect of λανθάνειν (*MS* A.3.a), "it has escaped your notice".

a9 τιμιώτερον: Neuter, "a ... thing"; more follow.

51b1

ἐν μείζονι μοίρᾳ: The noun sometimes means "share of respect due to one"; so here "held in greater esteem".

b3-4 θωπεύειν: "flatter", "lick the boots of", "cajole".

χαλεπαίνουσαν: "when it is vexed".

b4 ἃ ἂν κελεύῃ: Indefinite clause (*MS* D.3), another at b10.

b5-6 ἐάν clause: *MS* D.2.

ἐάντε ... ἐάντε ... ἐάντε: With the first two, "whether ... or", supply προστάττῃ; the third, with the subjunctive verb made explicit, may be translated by "and if"; this clause is picked up by ποιητέον ταῦτα.

δεῖσθαι: Passive infinitive of δεῖν, "to tie up, imprison".

b6-7 τρωθησόμενον: "to be wounded", future participle passive of τιτρώσκειν.

b7ff. ποιητέον ...: On these verbal adjectives see *MS* B.

b10 κελεύῃ singular: see on 47e9-48a1.

51c1

πείθειν: Supply δεῖ, implicit in the clutch of verbal adjectives at b7ff., cf. *MS* B.4.

ᾗ ... πέφυκε: Literally "as [ᾗ adverbial] the right naturally is", i.e. "in a manner properly in accord with the true nature of right"; πέφυκε is the perfect (*MS* A.3.a) of φύειν (~ φύσις, "nature"), used intransitively.

51c6-52a3

"We Laws make it possible for anyone who feels dissatisfied with us to take up residence elsewhere. To stay put is tantamount to approval, and imposes an obligation to obey."

Vocabulary
Verbs

ἀπ-αγορεύειν	forbid, veto
ἀρέσκειν	(with dative) be pleasing/ congenial to, satisfy
ἐπι-τάττειν	give instructions, lay down
δι-οικεῖν	administer, govern
μετ-οικεῖν	be a resident alien
μετα-διδόναι	give a share of/ in (genitive)
Adverbs	
ἐκεῖσε	thither, to that place
ἐμποδών	(standing) in one's path, presenting an obstacle

Aids to comprehension

51c7

ἡμᾶς (... δρᾶν): "to us", cf. on 50e6-7.

51d1

ὧν: Relative attraction, τούτων ἃ ...; cf. on 43d3.

d2-3 προ-αγορεύομεν has to wait for a while for its infinitive, ἐξεῖναι (~ impersonal ἔξεστι; noun ἐξουσία) at d5: "we proclaim publicly ... that it is possible/ permissible".

τῷ .. πεποιηκέναι: Articular infinitive (*MS* C.2, 3, 5; id. A.3.a), dative of means, "by the fact that we have created the possibility/ opportunity, made it permissible ..."

Ἀθηναίων τῷ βουλομένῳ: ὁ βουλόμενος is regularly used in the sense "anybody who wishes".

d3-4 ἐπειδὰν ...: Indefinite clause (*MS* D.3; more at 51d4, d5, e1, e2, e4-5, 52a1-2) with aorist subjunctives, "whenever he has officially come of age [δοκιμάζεσθαι, "be reviewed on having one's name entered in the deme-register" at the age of 18] and has seen ..."

τὰ ... πράγματα: i.e. the <workings of> the city's/ civic administration.

d5 λαβόντα: There is now a switch to a (more formal) accusative and infinitive construction with ἐξεῖναι, "that he should, having ..."

d7-8 ἐάντε (cf. *MS* D.2) ... ἐάντε: "whether ... or"; see on 51b5-6.

ἀποικίαν: "colony" (viz. an Athenian colony, ctr. μετοικία, "settlement in a foreign city").

εἰ μὴ ἀρέσκοιμεν: Explaining the wish to leave Athens behind, "supposing that/ in the event that we were not to ...", cf. *MS* E.2.

51e2

ὃν τρόπον: A common expression, "the way in which".

e3 τἆλλα: i.e. τὰ ἄλλα, "in all other respects".

e4 τοῦτον: An emphatic "this individual".

ὡμολογηκέναι: Perfect infinitive (*MS* A.3.b) of ὁμολογεῖν.

ἔργῳ: *"ipso facto"*, by his act of staying put.

e5 ποιήσειν: Cf. on 50c6-7, and below e7.

μή not οὐ: "anyone who ..."

τριχῇ: "in three ways", "on three counts".

e6-7 γεννηταῖς ... τροφεῦσι: (supply here οὐ πείθεται) "his procreators" (γεννητής, from γεννᾶν, cf. on 50d2-3) ... "his nurturers" (τροφεύς, from τρέφειν).

e8 εἰ ... ποιοῦμεν: "if there is anything we aren't doing right".

57

e8-52a2 προτιθέντων ...: Genitive absolute, "though we set before him <an alternative> and do not brutally dictate that he does what we tell him, but rather allow [ἐφ-ιέναι] him ..."

52a2

δυοῖν θάτερα: δυοῖν is genitive *dual* of δύο, θάτερα = τὰ ἔτερα, a plural frequently employed to indicate one of two alternative courses of action.
πείθειν: For the point about persuasion see *Theaetetus* 166a1ff.
a3 οὐδέτερα: See on 44d8.

<h1 style="text-align:center">52a3-53a8</h1>

"Socrates, you of all people have to stand by your agreement, in view of the way you have conducted yourself all your life; and consider your attitude on the occasion of your trial".

Vocabulary

Nouns

αἰτία, ἡ	accusation, charge
ἀποδημία, ἡ	journey away from home, abroad
ἐπιθυμία, ἡ	desire
συνθήκη, ἡ	agreement, compact
φυγή, ἡ	flight, exile
τεκμήριον, τό	item of evidence; plural, (body of) evidence, proof

Adjectives

τυφλός	blind
χωλός	lame

Verbs

παρα-βαίνειν	transgress, violate, break
πολιτεύεσθαι	function, conduct oneself as a citizen
στρατεύεσθαι	go on military service
ἀπατᾶν	deceive
ἀπο-δημεῖν	absent oneself from one's home, travel abroad
ἐπι-δημεῖν	stay at home
ἐπι-νοεῖν	intend
προ-αιρεῖσθαι	prefer
συν-τίθεσθαι	(middle, with infinitive) covenant, agree to

Adverbs
ἅπαξ   once, on a single occasion
διαφερόντως   to an exceptional degree, + genitive
("compared with"); or translate: to a
greater degree than ...
σφόδρα   vehemently, strongly
Preposition
ἄνευ   (with genitive) without

Aids to comprehension
52a3
ταύταις δή ...: "It is to *these* ... then ...", cf. 49e9.
a4 ἐνέξεσθαι serves as future infinitive *passive* of ἐν-έχεσθαι, "be held in", "be liable to".
εἴ-περ: "if actually", "if really".
ποιήσεις: See on 46a6-7.
a5 ἐν τοῖς: Again at a7; see on 43c7-8.
a6 διὰ τί δή; *"Why?"*, cf. 43c4.
a7 καθάπτοιντο: καθ-άπτεσθαι with genitive means "fasten on to", hence "lay into", "reprimand severely".
a8 ὡμολογηκώς: Perfect participle of ὁμολογεῖν, *MS* A.3.b; ... ὁμολογίαν: cf. on 46e1.
τυγχάνω: Cf. on 47b3; "had actually/ as a matter of fact ..."

52b1
ὅτι: See on 50c1.
b3-4 γάρ: "for otherwise", as quite often.
ἄν ... ποτε: "you would never be a resident <in Athens> all this time", the imperfect (cf. the note on 43b3-4) stressing the fact that this is a *continuing* state of affairs.
καὶ οὔτ' ... ἐξῆλθες: An abrupt switch to plain statements of fact (cf. ἐποίησω, ἔλαβεν).
b5 ἐπὶ θεωρίαν: "to be a spectator at a festival/ games" (like the Isthmian), but with a suggestion too of the notion of "seeing the world outside", cf. Solon the Athenian in Herodotus 1.30.1.
b6 ὅτι μὴ ἅπαξ εἰς Ἰσθμόν: It can hardly be doubted that these words are genuine, but their non-appearance in two of the three families of Plato MSS cannot be due to mere accident: their excision may go back ultimately to a feeling that the single journey specified here was not consistent with the (wholly general) observation on Socrates' stay-at-home habits in *Phaedrus* 230c6ff.
ὅτι μή after a negative clause is an idiomatic way of saying "except".

ἄλλοσε οὐδαμόσε: "to no (~ any) other place".

b7 στρατευσόμενος: Future participle expressing purpose, "to ..." Socrates' military service: *Apology* 28e2ff.

b8-9 ἐπιθυμία ... εἰδέναι: "desire of *x*, to know <about *x*>", the infinitive being added "epexegetically"; we might prefer to say "desire to know about *x*".

εἰδέναι (form: *MS* A.2) here means "to get to know about by direct observation".

52c1-2

ἡροῦ: "chose", here "chose in preference", like προαιρεῖσθαι (cf. 52e6).

καθ᾽ ἡμᾶς: Cf. d5-6 below, and expressions such as κατὰ τοὺς νόμους, "according to the rule of law".

πολιτεύσεσθαι: See on 50c6-7, and cf. d5 below.

c2 τά τε ἄλλα καί here means "and in particular" (cf. on ἄλλως τε καί at 50b7), the step about to be specified providing a sure sign of his satisfaction with the laws of the Athenian state.

c3 παῖδας .. ἐποιήσω: Cf. on 45d5.

ὡς with participle (genitive absolute) supplies the alleged rationale behind this act: "on the ground that ...", "in the conviction that..."

c4 ἔτι τοίνυν: "What is more". For ἔτι see on 44b9-10; τοίνυν here is not inferential (as it is elsewhere in *Crito*) but transitional, "further".

δίκῃ: "trial".

φυγῆς τιμήσασθαι: "to propose for yourself the penalty [τίμημα, "estimate", hence "the penalty fixed"] of exile", τιμᾶσθαι being a technical term for self-assessment of the punishment to be imposed by a court of law; φυγῆς is genitive of price or value.

c5-6 ἀκούσης τῆς πόλεως ... ἑκούσης: See on 48e3.

c6-7 ἐκαλλωπίζου ὡς ...: "put on a fine show of not being ...".

ἀγανακτῶν εἰ δέοι: "be indignant εἰ" is more naturally translated by our "... that": "at having to ...", cf. 43b10-11 above; optative because the leading verb is past, cf. *MS* E.3.

τεθνάναι: See on 43c9-d1.

c7 ὡς ἔφησθα: See *Apology* 37c4ff.

c8 πρό: See on 48d5-6.

c9 ἐντρέπῃ: ἐν-τρέπεσθαι, with genitive, = "pay heed to", "have regard/ respect for".

52d1

φαυλότατος: "meanest", "lowest".

d2-3 ἀποδιδράσκειν: See on 50a7.

παρά: "in contravention of" (cf. παρα-βαίνεις at e1 below), opp. καθ᾽ "in accordance with".

d5 ὡμολογηκέναι: Perfect infinitive (*MS* A.3.b) of ὁμολογεῖν.

d6 ἔργῳ ἀλλ' οὐ λόγῳ: We would say (agreed ...) "by your actions rather than by your words".

d6-7 φῶμεν ... ὁμολογῶμεν: Deliberative subjunctives (*MS* D.6(iv)).

ἄλλο τι ἤ: See on 50a9; cf. below d9.

d9 ἂν φαῖεν: ἄν is sometimes found at the head of a short utterance possessing the status of a light parenthesis, not regarded as constituting a separate clause; a Demosthenic example runs τί οὖν, ἄν τις εἴποι ...;

d9-52e1 πρὸς ἡμᾶς αὐτούς: "contracted with us personally". There is no ducking this issue: Socrates bound himself to obey the laws of his city, and they are there to prove it.

52e3

βουλεύσασθαι: Aorist, "come to a decision', "make up your mind".

e6 Λακεδαίμονα: See Nan Dunbar's note on Aristophanes, *Birds* 1281-83.

53a1

εὐνομεῖσθαι: "be regulated by good laws", "have model legal systems".

a2 βαρβάρων: "non-Greek", "foreign".

ἐλάττω: Literally "in respect of fewer <occasions>", cf. on 46c3-5.

a3 ἀνάπηροι: "physically handicapped", "disabled".

a5 δῆλον ὅτι: "evidently", "obviously" (sometimes written δηλονότι, cf. on 47b8), coming in emphatically at the close of the period: "... and we the laws — that's obvious!".

a5-6 πόλις .. ἄνευ νόμων together, "a city without laws".

a6 νῦν .. δή: *"now"* — in the face of all of these considerations.

ἐμμενεῖς is a future (cf. on 46a6-7).

ὡμολογημένοις: Perfect participle passive (*MS* A.5) of ὁμολογεῖν.

a6-7 ἐὰν ... πείθῃ: See *MS* D.2.

γε ... γε: "yes" (<you will>, if ...); then "at least".

καταγέλαστός .. ἔσῃ: "you'll be laughed to scorn", cf. on 45e5-6.

53a9-54b2

"If you do the wrong thing you will endanger your friends. Where will you go, and what kind of reception can you expect? You will be suspect in any law-abiding city. Your children will suffer more by your escape than by your death."

Vocabulary

Nouns

ἀκολασία, ἡ	licentiousness, lack of moral discipline, immoral behaviour
ἀταξία, ἡ	disorder
πολιτεία, ἡ	government, constitution
δικαστής, ὁ	juryman, judge

Adjectives

ἀνόητος	thoughtless, witless, mindless
κόσμιος	decent, law-abiding
λοιπός	left over, remaining

Verbs

ἀπο-λαύειν	enjoy an advantage, have the benefit of
τολμᾶν	dare, have the audacity to
εὐωχεῖσθαι	enjoy sumptuous entertainment, feast

Adverbs

γελοίως	ludicrously
ἐγγύς	(superlative ἐγγύτατα) close by, in the vicinity

Preposition

ἕνεκα	(with genitive, usually postpositive) for the sake of

Aids to comprehension
53a9-10
δή: See on 47a2.

ταῦτα ... τούτων: παρα-βάς is aorist, ἐξ-αμαρτάνων present participle: "if you have these contraventions behind you, and if you commit any of these offences".

ἐργάσῃ with two accusatives (so 54c4-5), as in English; cf. on 50e6-7, 51c7.

53b1-2
γε, laying stress on the preceding verb, may be represented by "will be exposed to danger, the danger of ..."

καί: as well as you yourself.

φεύγειν ~ φυγή "exile".

b3 ἀπολέσαι like ἀποβαλεῖν, "lose".

σχεδόν τι: See on 46b8.

πρῶτον μέν: Picked up by ἀλλ' ... in d1, cf. on 50d1-2.

ἐάν clause: *MS* D.2; more at 54a8-10.

b4-5 Θήβαζε [for -ασδε, cf. Ἀθήναζε] .. Μέγαράδε: "to Thebes .. to Megara".
Suffix -δε + accusative = "to" a locality.

b5 πολέμιος: A state-enemy, as opposed to ἐχθρός, a personal enemy.

b6 τούτων: Emphatic third person pronoun, *"their"*.

ὅσοι-: "all who", cf. on 46b2-3.

b7 ὑπο-βλέψονται: "will eye you with suspicion".

διαφθορέα: Agent noun -εύς, "destroyer", "corrupter".

b8-c1 βεβαιώσεις ... δοκεῖν: βεβαιοῦν = "render βέβαιον, firm, secure": "you will confirm for the jurymen their opinion, with the result that it is thought that they ...", i.e. "you will confirm the judges in their opinion — their opinion being as a result that they ..." The legal details are spelled out (and not only here) to Socrates in an appropriately long-winded fashion.

53c1

ὅστις with indicative. "a person who ..."

c2 που: "one must imagine".

νέων γε ...: The particle highlights the vulnerability of (and concern for) this element of the population. Recall the charge brought against Socrates, spelled out in *Apology* 24b8ff.

c3 πότερον (ἤ comes at c5): Cf. on 46c8.

c5 πλησιάσεις: πλησιάζειν with dative = "consort/ associate (closely) with" (~ adverb πλησίον, "in intimate contact, close proximity").

c6 ἀναισχυντήσεις (-εῖν) with participle, "have the impudence (ἀναισχυντία) to ..."

τίνας λόγους comes in easily on the heels of the element -λεγ- in the preceding participle.

c7 ἦ (not ἤ): Cf. on 43a1.

ὡς: "to the effect that".

c8 ἄξιον neuter: cf. on 51a9.

c8-9 τὰ νόμιμα καὶ οἱ νόμοι: One may think of νόμιμα as observances or standards of conduct sanctioned by usage, νόμοι as formally codified laws (cf. *Laws* 793a on τὰ καλούμενα ὑπὸ τῶν πολλῶν ἄγραφα νόμιμα): "the usages and institutions of law".

c9-d1 ἄσχημον [neuter singular of adjective ἀσχήμων-ονος] ... πρᾶγμα: "that this whole Socrates-affair will appear discreditable". πρᾶγμα, "business", is here, as often in various applications, derogatory.

οἴεσθαί γε χρή (again in 54b1-2): "Yes, one has to think so!", "You/ one must surely think that!".

ἀλλ᾽: "but will you rather ...?"

53d2

ἀπ-αρεῖς: This is the future of ἀπ-αίρειν, "lift/ carry off", used intransitively in the sense "take off".

d3 γὰρ δή: δή reinforces γάρ in a confident statement of fact: "because beyond a doubt".

d5 ἀπεδίδρασκες: See on 50a7.

σκευήν .. τινα περι-θέμενος: "having put on some form of get-up/ disguise" (σκευή ~ ἐν-σκευάζεσθαι d6, "dress oneself up in").

d6 διφθέραν: "leather jerkin".

οἷα: Qualitative relative, cf. on 44b8-9.

δή imparts a note of disparagement; best represented by a snigger.

εἰώθασιν: A third person plural perfect: *MS* A.3.b.

d7 σχῆμα ... μεταλλάξας: μετ-αλλάττειν = "take in exchange, swap, alter", σχῆμα = "form, configuration, outward appearance".

d8 ὅτι: We have to wait for the verb of saying: e2.

σμικροῦ ... ὄντος: Genitive absolute; another at 54a6.

53e1

ὡς τὸ εἰκός: See on 45d3.

γλίσχρως: Sarcastic: "glutinously", hence "clingingly", "greedily". There is a variant reading (οὕτως) αἰσχρῶς [~ 54c2] (uncial Λ miscopied as Α, then a bit of quiet tidying-up).

e2 οὐδεὶς ὃς ἐρεῖ; "<is there> nobody who will say?", "will there be nobody to remark?".

ἴσως: "perhaps <there will be nobody>".

ἄν: i.e. ἐάν, *MS* D.2.

e3 εἰ δὲ μή: i.e. in the event that you *do* annoy somebody: εἰ δὲ μή is a regular way of saying "otherwise", even when a preceding condition has been put in negative form.

ἀκούσῃ: Cf. on 51a1-2.

e4 ὑπ-ερχόμενος: "going/ getting under", i.e. "insinuating oneself into favour with", "ingratiating oneself with". When this particular verb is used metaphorically the normal contemporary prose practice of substituting parts of ἰέναι in the imperfect, the moods of the present, and the present participle of ἔρχομαι and compounds thereof (cf. *MS* D.7) is set aside.

δή in issuing a solemn admonition: "you may be sure", "be warned".

βιώσῃ: Future (middle form) of βιοῦν, "you'll live your life".

e5 τί: i.e. τί ἄλλο ...

e6 ἀποδεδημηκώς: Perfect participle of ἀπο-δημεῖν, *MS* A.3.a.

54a2-3

ἀλλὰ δή: "But you will say of course", introducing and anticipating a possible argument on the other side.

ἵνα ...: Final clause (another at 54a5), *MS* D.4.

a3 τί: "in what respect?" here means "by what means?".

a4 ἀγαγών: Cf. on 45a7-8.

a5 ἀπολαύσωσιν: Sarcastic.

... οὖ: Supply "won't happen".

αὐτοῦ: Adverbial: "right here", in Athens.

a6-7 θρέψονται καὶ παιδεύσονται here serve as future *passives;* cf. on 52a4.

μή not οὐ: the participle harbours a condition.

γάρ: "<Yes they will>, because ..." (cf. on 50c1).

a8 πότερον (cf. note on 46c8) here prefaces alternatives headed by "if"/ "if δέ".

a9 εἰς ῎Αιδου: "to Hades' <realm>", a common ellipse; cf. 54b5, and also 54c7.

a10-b1 εἴπερ: See on 52a4; γε reinforces this word.

... ὄφελος ...: See on 46a2-3.

ἐπιτηδείων naturally takes the case of the preceding participle.

54b3-d2

"Put what is right first, and do not incur our wrath or that of the powers below. And don't let Crito talk you round".

Vocabulary

Verbs

ἄρχειν	rule
ὑπο-δέχεσθαι	receive, welcome
ἀπο-λογεῖσθαι	plead in one's own defence
Adverb	
εὐμενῶς	[adj. -ής] in a friendly, well-meaning fashion, with goodwill

Aids to comprehension

54b3

ἀλλ': See on 44b6-7.

τροφεῦσι: See on 51e6-7.

b4 περὶ πλείονος ποιοῦ: See on 44c3.

τὸ ζῆν: Articular infinitive, *MS* C.

b5 πρό: "setting <these> before", cf. on 48d5-6.

ἵνα: Final clause, *MS* D.4.

b6 ἐκεῖ: "in the other world", opp. ἐνθάδε "in this".

b6-9 οὔτε γὰρ ... ἔσται: οὔτε in 6 corresponds to οὔτε in 8; in 7-8, ἄμεινον ... οὐδὲ δικαιότερον οὐδὲ ὁσιώτερον, οὐδέ may be translated as "or" in both cases; the second οὐδέ in 8 joins σοι in 7 to ἄλλῳ. So: "because if you take this course it does not seem to be better or ... or ..., for you here, or for any other of ... either, nor will it be better for you ..."

δικαιότερον .. ὁσιώτερον: i.e. more in accordance with what is righteous <in the human sphere> ... more in accordance with what is righteous <in dealing with the gods>. (*Gorgias* 507b: one who is σώφρων in dealing properly with his fellow-men δίκαι᾽ ἂν πράττοι, in dealing properly with the gods ὅσια — piety being regarded as a contractual obligation.)

b8 τῶν σῶν: i.e. your friends and others close to you.

b9-c1 νῦν: "as things stand", cf. on 44d8.

ἠδικημένος: Perfect participle passive (*MS* A.5) of ἀδικεῖν.

ἄπει: Future of ἀπ-ιέναι, "you will go away, depart".

54c1

ἐάν clause (cf. c2): see *MS* D.2.

ἀπίῃς: Cf. *MS* D.7.

c4-5 κακὰ ἐργασάμενος τούτους: Cf. on 53a9-10.

c6 χαλεπανοῦμεν: Future of χαλεπαίνειν (cf. on 51b3-4), "will be angry" with (dative).

c7 ἐν ῞Αιδου: "in <the realm> of Hades", cf. on 54a9.

c8-d1 εἰδότες: Perfect participle, *MS* A.2.

καὶ ἡμᾶς: Probably "as well", that is to say, he would very likely try to accord the same treatment to the laws down below, hence the chilly reception.

τὸ σὸν μέρος: See on 50b2.

54d1

μή .. πείσῃ: A prohibition expressed by μή and third person aorist subjunctive (cf. *MS* D.6(ii)): "don't let ...".

54d3-e2

Has Crito anything to say now? He has not. Things must take their course, as "the god" directs.

Vocabulary
Noun
ἑταῖρος, ὁ   companion, comrade
Adverb
μάτην   in vain, to no purpose

Aids to comprehension

54d3

ἴσθι (again at d6) is imperative singular of εἰδέναι, *MS* A.2.

d4 οἱ κορυβαντιῶντες: A reference to Corybantic ritual in which some respectable Athenians took part (*Euthydemus* 277d): "people affected by the Corybantic bug [-ιᾶν: cf. for instance ὀφθαλμ-ιᾶν, "suffer from the condition ophthalmia"]": "... the Corybantes were a mythical group associated with the goddess Cybele, and the special feature of their cult was the drum- and pipe-music which induced a curative frenzy in those who were 'possessed' in the sense 'deranged'"", K.J. Dover on Plato, *Symposium* 215e1.

d5 αὕτη ... τούτων carry stress, "it is *this* ... of *these* words that ...", shutting out *all other* (τῶν ἄλλων) words.

ἠχή: An appropriate term for noise in the ears, and for the sound of αὐλοί.

βομβεῖ: "buzzes away" in me (my ears), as insistently one might say as a tinnitus, a condition often associated with an initial trauma but thereafter generally unrelated to external stimuli.

d6-7 ὅσα ... δοκοῦντα: See on 46e3.

ἐάν clause: *MS* D.2.

παρά: "in opposition to", a good legal-sounding preposition, cf. on 52d2-3.

d8 ὅμως μέντοι: Strongly put: "nevertheless, for all that".

τι .. πλέον ποιήσειν: "achieve something more" is an idiomatic way of saying "derive any advantage".

d9 ἀλλ': "on the contrary", "no".

54e1

ἔα (ἐᾶν): "let it be", "leave it at that"; cf. 48c2, and note on 45a1.

πράττωμεν: First person plural subjunctive (*MS* D.6.(i)) in the sense "let us ...".

e2 ὁ θεός: Cf. the closing words of *Apology*, 42a4-5.

ὑφ-ηγεῖται: "leads, conducts <us>" (~ ὑφηγητής, "guide").

SUGGESTIONS FOR FURTHER READING

Notable among annotated editions of *Crito* in English are those of J. Adam (2nd edn, Cambridge, 1891; with vocabulary, 1927) and J. Burnet (Oxford, 1924). *Four Texts on Socrates,* by T.G. and G.S. West (Ithaca, 1984), contains annotated translations of Plato's *Euthyphro, Apology* and *Crito,* and Aristophanes' *Clouds,* and also a critical bibliography.

Other works of interest:
Barker, A., 'Why did Socrates Refuse to Escape?', *Phronesis* 22 (1977), 13-28.
Gulley, N., *The Philosophy of Socrates* (London, 1968), 192-200.
Guthrie, W.K.C., *History of Greek Philosophy* vol.iv (Cambridge, 1975), 93-101.
Irwin, T., *Plato's Ethics* (Oxford, 1995).
Santas, G.X., *Socrates* (London, 1979), 10-56.
Woozley, A.D., 'Socrates on Disobeying the Law', in Vlastos, G. (ed.), *The Philosophy of Socrates* (New York, 1971), 299-318.
— *Law and Obedience: the Arguments of Plato's Crito* (London, 1979; includes a translation).